History's Outrageous Oddities

A "Twist In Time" Book

History's Outrageous Oddities

A *"Twist In Time"* Book

Bill Coate

Twist In Time Books
Fresno, California

Copyright © 2007 Bill Coate
All Rights Reserved

Printed in the United States of America

No part of this book may be used or reproduced in any manner whatsoever without written permission except in the case of brief quotations embodied in critical articles and reviews. Please do not participate in or encourage electronic piracy of copyrighted materials in violation of the author's rights.

For more information, address:
Twist In Time Books
1920 Julius St., Madera, CA 93637
(559) 647-2036 or (559) 706-5297

Twist In Time materials may be purchased for educational, business, or sales promotional use. For information please contact: Marketing Department, Twist In Time Books at the above address and phone numbers.

Cover Design © Book and Cover Layout
Robert L. Oldham / August Publishing Group

Printing
Quill Driver Books/World Dancer Press, Inc.

ISBN 10: 0-9768252-2-8
ISBN 13: 978-0-9768252-2-7
LCCN 2005936415

To Mary,
Who Gives Unselfishly
To Her
Husband,
Children,
And
Grandchildren

TABLE OF CONTENTS

INTRODUCTION   *iii*

"HISTORY'S OUTRAGEOUS ODDITIES" TWISTS IN TIME

EARLY AMERICAN ODDITIES WITH A TWIST   1

CRUEL AND UNUSUAL PUNISHMENT 3
PURITAN MORALITY WANED OVER TIME 5
REBECCA'S FATEFUL ATLANTIC CROSSING 8
NEW HAMPSHIRE'S PINE TREE RIOT 10
REVENGE AT CHRISTMAS 12
FROM PAINT BRUSHES TO POLITICS 14
THE GRIM REAPER DENIED 16
THE SCAR THAT NEVER HEALED 18
HOW THE AMERICAN REVOLUTION BROKE FAMILY BONDS .20
BENJAMIN FRANKLIN'S THANKSGIVING LEGACY 22
THE MARYLAND PARSON AND HIS LITTLE WHITE LIE 24
THE BROUHAHA OVER THE BONES OF DANIEL BOONE 26
BOYS GO WILD AT HARVARD 29
GONE BUT NOT FORGOTTEN 31
THE PERSONIFICATION OF AMERICA 33
THE AMERICAN IDOL WHO DIDN'T TELL
EVERYTHING HE KNEW 35
THE FOUNDING FATHER WITH A WANDERING EYE 37
SEGREGATION ASSAULTED IN EARLY AMERICA 39
BLACKMAIL, BRIBERY, AND THE PRESIDENCY 41
BEN'S BOOZE DID THE TRICK 44

PRESIDENTIAL ODDITIES WITH A TWIST   47

DID WASHINGTON TELL THE TRUTH ABOUT HIS AGE? 49
WASHINGTON'S FINAL SECRET 51
THE SCOUNDREL WHO ALMOST BECAME PRESIDENT 53
JOHN QUINCY ADAMS IS CAUGHT
IN A COMPROMISING POSITION 56
THE HIDDEN MEANING OF "HAIL TO THE CHIEF" 58
HOW DIRTY TRICKS COST ONE MAN THE PRESIDENCY 60
WHY ANDREW JACKSON MARRIED ANOTHER MAN'S WIFE ..62

TABLE OF CONTENTS

OLD HICKORY'S BARNYARD SYMBOL 64
THE TWO FACES OF A WAR PROTESTER 67
DID ABRAHAM LINCOLN HAVE SECOND THOUGHTS? 70
RECORDING HISTORY UNDER THE PRESIDENT'S FEET 72
LINCOLN THE LEXICOGRAPHER 74
HOW CIVIL PRIDE GAVE BIRTH TO MEMORIAL DAY 76
THE VICE PRESIDENT WHO NEVER MADE IT HOME 78
HOW FREE LOVE EXTRACTED ITS POUND OF FLESH 80
POLITICAL TREACHERY 83
THE PRESIDENT WHO ROCKED THE CRADLE 85
DRAMA FOLLOWS LINCOLN TO WASHINGTON 88
ONE MAN'S COSTLY EPITAPH 90
TAFT'S LEGACY WENT BEYOND THE BATHROOM 92
TEDDY ROOSEVELT'S COFFEE HOUSE PROVERB 94
TEDDY ROOSEVELT'S DOUBLE WHAMMY 96
HOW A DREAM ALMOST COST A PRESIDENT HIS LIFE 98
INEBRIATION AT LINCOLN'S INAUGURATION 100

CIVIL WAR ODDITIES WITH A TWIST   103

A REBEL IN THE WHITE HOUSE 105
GENERAL GRANT READ THE SIGNS 107
GETTYSBURG AND CANDY MAN 109
HOW JACKSON LOST A BATTLE BUT MADE
A NAME FOR HIMSELF 111
A WOMAN SUCCEEDS WHILE THE MEN DAWDLE 113
YOU CAN'T TAKE THE SOUTH OUT OF THE BOY 115
DEVOTION PAYS DIVIDENDS 117
FIGHTING JOE WHEELER SERVED TWO MASTERS 120
ONE SOLDIER'S LEGACY FROM MISSIONARY RIDGE 122
THE BULL RUN "RUNNERS" 124
TOO MANY PIGS FOR THE TEATS 126
THE KILLER RETURNED TO THE SCENE OF THE CRIME 128
THE LUCK OF THE IRISH 130
TEXANS WHO COULD NOT BE THROTTLED 132
THE THIRD TIME HAD NO CHARM 134
THE WEEK NEW YORK WENT CRAZY 136
POLITICAL RIVALRY WITH LINCOLN LASTED TO THE END ..139
TRIFLING WITH OLD GLORY 141
NO MERCY FOR MARY SURRATT......................................143

TABLE OF CONTENTS

WILD WEST ODDITIES WITH A TWIST   *145*

THE TEN COMMANDMENTS OF STAGE COACH TRAVEL 147
FRONTIER JUSTICE WAS SWIFT AND SURE 149
HOW SAMUEL CLEMENS PICKED MARK TWAIN 150
INSIDER INFORMATION AT THE
CONSTITUTIONAL CONVENTION 152
THE PREACHER WHO SOUGHT HIS DUE 154
CHINESE HURDLE THE SIERRA NEVADA 156
HELL HATH NO FURY 158
IN MEMORY OF THORNBURGH 160
ROBES OF RIGHTEOUSNESS FELL IN UTAH 162
THE PRICE OF DISCOVERING YOSEMITE VALLEY 164
CHARACTER BUILDING ON THE FRONTIER 166
CUSTER AND THE ROOSTER 168
MOSES SCHALLENBERGER'S MOUNTAIN MONUMENT 170
BUFFALO BILL'S ELUSIVE HONOR 172
SIDESTEPPING TRAGEDY ON A MISSISSIPPI RIVERBOAT 174
RANK HAD ITS PRIVILEGES 176
SHAKING HANDS AT THE WRONG TIME 178
WILLIAM TODD'S PIG 180

MODERN ODDITIES WITH A TWIST   *183*

HOCKEY'S BLOODY ST. PATRICK'S DAY 185
GENERAL PATTON LOST THE RACE 187
AMERICA'S ANNUAL HALLOWEEN SEANCE 190
THE PRESIDENT'S DAUGHTER HAD THE LAST WORD 192
THE REAL LEGACY OF PEARL HARBOR 194
THE NEW YORK TIMES EATS ITS WORDS 196
FOR THE LOVE OF THE GAME 198
HOW THELMA HIT THE BIG TIME 200
JOHN JACOB ASTOR MAKES A FATAL CHOICE 202
IN DEFENSE OF JOE MCCARTHY 204
TEDDY ROOSEVELT AND THE SHAH OF IRAN 206
THE ARMY UNLEASHES A SECRET WEAPON ON BOSTON 208
THE GOVERNOR WHO COULDN'T WIN 210
THE KING, THE KAISER, AND THE CZAR 212
THE MAN WHO NEVER, NEVER, NEVER GAVE UP 214
HOW AMERICA BEAT FRANCE AT THE WORLD'S FAIR 216

TABLE OF CONTENTS

IN PRAISE OF THOMAS CRAPPER 218
NEGLECT OF THE TROOPS PROMPTS
A "ROUND ROBIN" REVIEW 219
CHICANERY AT THE SMITHSONIAN INSTITUTION 221
MAINTAINING THE DIGNITY OF CHEF BOYARDEE 223
THE DAY THE U.S. GOVERNMENT LOOKED
A GIFT HORSE IN THE MOUTH 225
ONE WRITER'S WORDS BOUNCE BACK TO HAUNT HIM 227
PANCHO VILLA TO THE RESCUE 229

OLD WORLD ODDITIES WITH A TWIST   *231*

VENERATION TOOK ITS TOLL 233
TURKISH DELIGHT IN VIENNA FAILED
TO SAVE THE QUEEN 235
BOBBY LIVES ON 237
THE LADY LEFT A LEGACY 239
FAME HAD ITS PRICE 241
PARLIAMENT GOT AN EARFUL 243
OLIVER CROMWELL LOST HIS HEAD 245
THE GERMAN WHO FOUGHT HIS FAMILY 247

BIBLIOGRAPHY   *249*

INDEX   *261*

INTRODUCTION

This third book in the "Twist in Time" series was born out of the conviction that the historian must mediate history, or s/he will become a luxury that society can ill afford.

The author has been a historian for thirty-five years. He has earned a B.A. and an M.A. in history and has taught the discipline in public schools since 1972.

Over these past three decades, one thing has become abundantly clear to the writer. Although almost everyone has an inner love for the past, most of us cannot abide a steady diet of Master's theses or Doctoral dissertations, as pivotal as they may be.

What lies closes to our hearts are good narrative histories—stories well told. We long for poignant accounts of the past, written with flair that holds our attention. We are not a nation of monograph readers, but we do love lively accounts of our yesteryears.

The impact of these simple truths hit the author with full force when he first began his career teaching U.S. history in junior high school. It took just a day or two to understand that if he was going to engage these young minds to any significant degree, he would have to become a good story teller. His teenage students were not about to sit still for dull lectures and meaningless assignments.

By the same token, when he later became an adjunct history instructor at the college level, things were not much different. His students responded with enthusiasm to any attempt to lift them above the normally dry, dusty monologues by using animated accounts of the American pageant.

Then twelve years ago he was challenged by a local television station to bring his stories to a broader audience. The station manager envisioned a short run of historical vignettes that would serve to add something different to the nightly news. It proved to be a most exciting experience for the teacher as historian.

He dipped into his haversack of history for some stories that had just a bit of irony—a little twist in time—thus the name, "Twist in Time." The response was immediate and sustained. People called the station to express their approval of a history segment that was part of the nightly news. They further indicated appreciation for history lessons that came without ivory towered condescension. In short, our "Twist in Time" made the viewer feel connected to history without having to endure a lecture.

Weeks melted into months and months into years, and now here we are, more than a decade later, not only bringing our stories to a growing television audience but inviting history lovers from across the country to join us as we explore the ironic touches of our American past in another "Twist in Time" book.

The reader will quickly see that no era of American history is immune from those strange twists of fate that save us from our dogmatic slumbers and give us cause for reflection. From Jefferson, Adams, and Jackson to Babe Ruth and Adolph Hitler, our stories cover the broad spectrum of our nation's political, social, and economic past.

It is our hope that readers will find these "Twists" both enjoyable and worthwhile.

Bill Coate
Madera, California

Early American Oddities
With A Twist

CRUEL AND UNUSUAL PUNISHMENT

Salem Witchhunt Trial Judge

Citizens of the United States are protected against cruel and unusual punishment by the Constitution. The need for such a shield came from the outrageous methods with which the English common law dealt with criminals. Our Founding Fathers didn't want to see anyone drawn and quartered or burned at the stake. Unfortunately, for Giles Corey, this prohibition against cruel and unusual punishment didn't come quite soon enough to save him from a horrible death at the hands of officials in colonial America.

Corey left Old England in the 17th century to settle in New England. He became a rather prosperous farmer who tried to do everything right. Giles and his wife, Martha, attended to all of the demands that Puritan society placed on them, including the obligatory attendance at divine services on Sunday. That's why he was so surprised when the authorities, accompanied by the preacher, came to take him to jail. He was accused of abusing two little girls who lived in the parsonage.

Nothing could have shocked Giles Corey any more

than this accusation. He had always been respectful of the parson and his family, including his young niece who had moved in with them. So outraged was he by the charges, that Giles refused to even enter a plea, and this placed him in an unenviable position. In those days before the Declaration of Independence and the Constitution, English common law prevailed, and that meant that Corey was caught on the horns of a dilemma. If he refused to enter a plea, he would have to undergo the ancient punishment of *"peine forte et dure."* In the face of his obdurate refusal to reply to the charges, he would face execution by being pressed to death.

On Monday, September 19, 1692, they took Corey from jail and led him to a site adjacent to the courthouse. When he refused one last time to enter a plea, he was stripped naked and made to lie between two boards. Heavy rocks were then placed upon his chest. Every hour more rocks were added, until finally he could hardly breathe.

At noon the next day, eighty year-old Giles Corey spoke his last words. "More rocks," he whispered, "more rocks." He wanted death to come quickly. When the executioner obliged him, Corey lapsed into a semi-conscious state, and his tongue was "pressed out of his mouth." As the Sheriff forced it back in again with his cane, Giles Corey mercifully departed this earth.

Ironically, watching the whole, dreadful spectacle was the Reverend Samuel Parris, whose daughter, Betty, and niece, Abigail Williams, had accused the old farmer of abuse by casting spells on them. You see, the two young cousins had started the Salem witchcraft hysteria, and Giles Corey was one of its victims.

Thus, in a strange twist in time, the shenanigans of these two girls in the 1692 Salem Witchhunt and the refusal of Giles Corey to dignify the town's insanity, laid the foundations for building America's safeguards against cruel and unusual punishment.

PURTIAN MORALITY WANED OVER TIME

William Bradford

It is almost impossible to remember the first Thanksgiving and the Mayflower without thinking of William Bradford. This Pilgrim leader was as firm in his beliefs as Plymouth Rock. He lived a life of unwavering opposition to those who were guilty of adultery, drunkenness, and Sabbath violations. He opposed anyone who was at variance with the ordinances of the Almighty. That's what makes his legacy so surprising.

William Bradford was born in Austerfield, England, in 1590. As an adult, he believed so strongly in living the pure life that he left the Church of England to join the Separatists, a branch of the Puritans. After a sojourn in Holland, Bradford and 101 other Separatists came to America in 1620, and started Plymouth Colony on Massachusetts Bay.

Bradford and his co-religionists first elected John Carver to be governor of the colony, but he died a few months later. The colonists then chose Bradford to be their governor, a position he held for 30 years.

During his tenure as governor, Bradford had to rule Plymouth Colony with an iron hand, both in secular and spiritual matters. That first winter in the New World, 1620-1621, was a terrible one. Freezing cold and disease took a grisly toll. Of the original 102 Pilgrims, Bradford had to bury 58 of them before spring. It was only through his strong leadership that the remainder survived to tend to matters of the soul.

Just as he nursed the tiny colony back to physical health, Bradford also saw to their spiritual welfare, which meant the Pilgrims lived abstemious religious lives. They worked hard, attended simple church services on Sunday, and observed all of the rules expected of God's elect.

Throughout his tenure, William Bradford would countenance no licentiousness, ungodly passions, drunkenness, revels, or carousing. On one occasion, he even broke up a street game of "stoole-ball," because it was frivolous and "against his conscience that they should play…."

Thus for three decades did William Bradford lead Plymouth Colony according to a strict moral code. He was observant to his duties as a Christian to the end, and his spirituality bore fruit for generations, especially among his offspring and their descendants. Then came the Twentieth century, and it all went to pot.

When William Bradford died in 1657, his mantle fell on his son, Thomas Bradford and his grandson, James Bradford. William's old Puritan ideals were even carried on to some extent in the fourth generation with his great-granddaughter, Mary Bradford. After her, however, there was a steady loosening of the moral code in the family, until by the time the 1960s rolled around, there was a complete meltdown.

For you see, by that time William Bradford's grandson, eight times removed, had come on the scene and made his own unique contribution to the social climate of the day—one that would have made his Bradford ancestor spin in his grave.

In a wild twist in time, the family lineage and Puritan legacy of William Bradford came to rest in the person of Hugh Hefner, who by his own admission rejected his strict religious heritage and invented "Playboy" instead. One has to wonder what Hefner would say to "Grandpa Bradford" if only he had the chance.

REBECCA'S FATEFUL ATLANTIC CROSSING

Pocahontas

    Rebecca was a beautiful and erudite, young woman of the 17th century. By the time she was in her early twenties, she had traveled the Atlantic, which in those days was no small accomplishment. In 1616, she and her husband caused quite a stir in London when King James I invited them to his court. The English royal family wanted to hear her stories of the New World.

    Rebecca regaled King James with fantastic tales of life in the new colony of Jamestown, Virginia. She told how disease and starvation had almost wiped out the first permanent English settlement in the New World. She related how the incredible young adventurer, Captain John Smith, had saved the colony by decreeing that those who did not work would not eat. The King and his court were completely taken with her intelligent, first-hand observations.

    Rebecca went on to enjoy the attention of London's high society for nearly a year, but then it all came to an abrupt end. Her husband decided that he wanted to make another trip to Jamestown. He had some ideas on how to render the colony more prosperous.

As Rebecca prepared to leave England, however, concerns for her health began to grow. The Trans-Atlantic voyage would take over two months, and she had developed a severe respiratory ailment, which the physicians could not cure. Nevertheless, in March 1617, she and her husband and their young son, Thomas, boarded a sailing ship bound for Virginia.

Within a day or two it became apparent that she would not survive the trip, so the ship returned to port long enough for Rebecca to be removed. Her husband obtained lodging with a friend and sought the services of a physician. Alas, there was nothing that could be done.

As she lay dying, Rebecca comforted her husband by reminding him that "All must die. Tis enough that the child liveth." At the age of 22, she gave up the ghost and was buried In Gravesend, England.

After Rebecca's funeral, her husband made provisions to leave his son in England while he returned to Jamestown. He had come up with a plan to finally gain prosperity from the New World. He would make the colonists self-sufficient by teaching them how to raise tobacco.

For you see, Rebecca's husband was John Rolfe, father of the American tobacco industry, and she was really Pocahontas, the famous Indian maiden who was supposed to have saved the life of Captain John Smith. When she married Rolfe in 1613, she was baptized and took the Christian name of Rebecca.

Then in a peculiar twist in time, Rolfe took his Indian bride to England to show her off while he was seeking funding for his tobacco scheme. Given her dynamism and courage, one has to wonder how Pocahontas might have further altered Jamestown's history had she lived to return.

NEW HAMPSHIRE'S PINE TREE RIOT

Pine Tree Flag

The Boston Massacre—The Boston Tea Party—The Stamp Act Revolt—these acts of disobedience that led to the Declaration of Independence are well known episodes on the pages of American History. They are not, however, the only examples of defiant outbursts of colonial frustration with British rule. In 1772, the royal governor of New Hampshire stirred the cauldron of discontent so furiously that it boiled over into a full fledged riot, and it was all over a tax on trees.

The conflict started when Governor John Wentworth, decided to collect a tax on the pine trees that were being cut by Ebenezer Mudgett, owner of a mill in South Weare, New Hampshire. On April 13, 1772, Wentworth sent the county sheriff and a deputy to either collect the tax or arrest the recalcitrant lumberman. Little did they know just how much support Mudgett had in his hometown.

By the time the sheriff and his deputy reached Weare night had fallen, so they got a room in Aaron Quimby's Inn, which was ironically called the Pine Tree Tavern. The innkeeper had no sooner registered his guests than he sent word that the King's men had come to Weare to deal with Mudgett. The news spread like wild fire, and within an hour, a mob of Weare residents was on its way to Quimby's Inn.

The protestors blackened their faces and then slipped into the inn and up to the sheriff's room. The lawman and his deputy were aroused from a deep sleep when the men burst into their room. In a moment the duo found themselves completely subdued.

One of the Weare tax protesters then produced a switch from a pine tree. While his cohorts held the two tax collectors by the arms and legs, the man with the switch applied it to their bare backs with great dexterity—one lash for every tree they wanted to tax.

When they were finished, the mob chased the two men out of town through a gauntlet of jeering, shouting townspeople. Then to add further insult, the lawmen's horses, with ears cropped and manes and tails shorn, were sent running after their owners.

Thus we see that a tax on tea and stamps was not the only source of outrage which American colonists directed toward their British overlords. In a surprising twist in time, the folks in Weare, New Hampshire, showed that Americans could get just as wrothy over their pine trees as they could their tea. Obviously, Boston did not have a monopoly on twisting the tail of the British Lion.

REVENGE AT CHRISTMAS

Washington Gets
His Revenge

In the winter of 1776, the American army was on the verge of collapse, having been driven from New York by the British in the first year of the American Revolution. General George Washington led his tattered troops in retreat across the Hudson River and plodded barefoot across New Jersey. It looked like the end had come, and this probably would have been the case, had it not been for a propitious Christmas celebration.

As Washington retreated southwest across New Jersey, an enemy who was intent on, not only destroying what was left of the American Army, but pillaging the countryside as well, followed him. New Jersey, with its well-tended farms, abundant supplies of food and livestock, and barrels of wine and beer, offered prime targets for the depredations of the hated Hessian invaders.

Finally Washington reached the Delaware River and crossed into Pennsylvania. His army was almost gone, but he had two trump cards to play. First, he knew his soldiers who remained were aching to exact retribution for the brutal conduct of King George's hired German soldiers, and second he surmised that the Hessians would "make a great deal of Christmas, and no doubt would drink a great deal of beer." Therefore, the General decided to move boldly.

He gave the Hessians plenty of time to drink their beer and conduct their Christmas revelry, then after recrossing the Delaware, he struck. The surprised, confused and hung-over Germans ran to an orchard where they surrendered to the vengeful Americans. It all happened in less than forty-five minutes. Twenty-one Hessians were killed and 90 wounded. The Americans took 900 prisoners while 500 escaped. Thus did Washington pull the remnants of the Continental Army from the abyss of defeat, for you see, the General had just defeated the Hessians at the famous battle of Trenton.

In a fateful twist in time, the Germans let down their guard and indulged themselves on Christmas Day, 1776. Not to be denied their traditional celebration of Christmas, especially with an abundance of beer at their disposal, the Hessians gave the American Revolution new life, just as the army was about to throw in the towel.

Their success at Trenton did not end the lean times for the Americans as they fought to throw off the yoke of British rule, but it did represent the beginning of the end, thanks to the determination of the Germans to have a Christmas party.

FROM PAINT BRUSHES TO POLITICS

George Washington

The year was 1772, and although revolution was in the air, two brothers were making their way from Philadelphia to Mount Vernon with their canvas and brushes to paint a portrait of George Washington. When they were through, they returned home, and the older sibling, Charles Willson Peale, took on the task of teaching the younger brother, James, how to paint. Unfortunately war interrupted the lessons and almost robbed the nation of a treasure trove of art.

Two years after their visit to Mount Vernon, the Peale brothers met George Washington again. This time, however, he had come to their hometown, Philadelphia, as a delegate to the Continental Congress. In 1775, he was appointed by that body to lead the colonial army in its struggle against the British. From there, Washington headed for Boston to take charge of the military, while the Peales continued their painting lessons.

For a few months, things went well for both the Peales and Washington. James was improving, and Washington's troops had chased the British out of Boston. Then came 1776. The British army moved down to take New York, and Washington shifted his troops south to check them. When he got there he found that he was facing a force twice his size and had to retreat from Long Island to Manhattan to New Jersey. That's when the Peales turned from painting to politics.

James was the first to join Washington's forces, and he was with him every step of the way as the British pounded the patriot army across New Jersey. By the time they reached the Delaware River, illness and desertion had reduced their

WWW.TWISTINTIME.COM

numbers by two-thirds. One observer called Washington's troops a "shadow army." It was at that point that Charles Willson Peale decided to lay down his paintbrush and join his brother in the struggle. All he had to do was find him.

Charles was on the West Bank of the Delaware looking for James when Washington's troops made the crossing. Peale had never seen such a motley accumulation of humanity in his life. As he walked among the exhausted troops, he could not believe his eyes. Most of the men were sick, hungry, and completely demoralized. Some carried the look of death as they sat on the frozen ground awaiting some miracle. For Charles the miracle would be in finding his brother.

As he went from man to man, they all had that "disfigured" look. Then he passed by one poor, suffering wretch who seemed to epitomize the state of the American army in 1776. "He had almost no clothes. He was in an old dirty blanket jacket, his beard long, and his face so full of sores that he could not clean it." Charles shook his head and passed him by, then he stopped and went back for a second look. Once more he thought his eyes deceived him, for you see, this pitiful creature was his own brother, James Peale!

Over the next few days, Charles nursed James to health, and then they both continued to serve in Washington's army until independence from Great Britain was won. After that they returned to painting and established a reputation. They and their offspring became known as the "Painting Peales," and Americans put them in the same category as Gilbert Stuart and John Singleton Copley.

In an unexpected twist in time, the Peales went on to establish their own school of art, and all because Charles Willson Peale saved his brother's life on that cold December morning on the banks of the Delaware River, while General George Washington was trying to figure out what to do.

THE GRIM REAPER DENIED

James Monroe

    The young, 18 year-old Lieutenant lay writhing in pain on the frozen ground of the orchard. The musket ball had grazed the left side of his chest and then his shoulder, injuring the axillary artery that brought blood to his arm. The wound bled profusely and began to drain life from the fallen soldier. If he died, not only would General George Washington lose a valuable aide, but also the young lad would never fulfill his destiny on the stage of history.

    When the Lieutenant had joined the army, the outlook had been sanguine. The British Redcoats had been chased out of Boston, to the cheers of Patriots from New Hampshire to Georgia. Then came those catastrophic losses in New York and the dreadful winter retreat across New Jersey. What had started out as a proud army of 20,000 had been reduced to a remnant of barely 3,000 ill-fed and poorly equipped troops who were huddling on the Pennsylvania side of the Delaware River, across from Trenton, New Jersey.

Then came those Christmas Eve orders from General Washington to recross the Delaware and surprise the enemy by retaking Trenton. The Lieutenant felt a surge of pride as he relayed the order to his men and prepared to move out.

Despite the freezing weather and the logistical nightmare of crossing the river in a storm, the Lieutenant and his men followed their commander. The wisdom of the plan bore fruit, as Washington's army surprised the Hessians completely.

As fate would have it, the enemy managed to roll out a cannon but was never able to fire on the Americans. The young Lieutenant and Captain William Washington, the General's cousin, rushed forward, seized the field piece, and turned it on the German mercenaries, who made a bee-line for a nearby orchard. Captain Washington and the Lieutenant followed.

For forty-five minutes, the orchard battle at Trenton, New Jersey, raged. After 21 Hessians had been killed and 90 wounded, 900 of King George's hired troops surrendered. The remaining 500 escaped into the countryside. Incredibly, given the intensity of the battle, no Americans were killed, and only four were wounded. One of these was the young Lieutenant.

For a few moments, the young officer's life hung in the balance. Then the army surgeon stumbled upon him. The medic stanched the flow of blood by sticking his index finger into the wound and applying pressure to the artery. By virtue of this life-saving measure, the Lieutenant was saved for posterity, for you see, that young officer was none other than James Monroe of Virginia. In a miraculous twist in time, Lieutenant Monroe was jerked back from the jaws of death at the Battle of Trenton in 1776, and lived to become the fifth President of the United States.

Forty years later he would raise his hand to take the oath of office, but he would do it slowly, for they never found that Hessian bullet that almost ended his life before it ever really got started.

THE SCAR
THAT NEVER HEALED

Andrew Jackson

Andrew Jackson was born in a backwoods settlement called the Waxhaws, on the border between North and South Carolina. He was made of stern, Scotch-Irish stock, which meant he was tough as nails and would submit to no insult—not even when threatened by the sword of a British army officer for refusing to shine his boots. The price for this teenager's granite resolve was a scar across his forehead, but in the end, the British paid dearly for the act.

The boy never knew his father, who died a few days before he was born, but he had two older brothers, Hugh and Robert, who did what they could to fill the void. While his siblings tried to eke out a living by farming the family plot, Andrew attended a local frontier school. He quickly acquired the reputation of being intelligent but fiery-tempered and willing to fight all comers.

When the lad was eight years old, he learned of the firing of the "shots heard round the world" at Lexington and Concord. By the time he was 13, that fight had reached North Carolina, as the Redcoats invaded the Waxhaws. The boy and his two brothers immediately joined the local militia. Hugh was killed, and Robert and Andrew were taken prisoner.

On the first night of his captivity, the British officer in charge ordered Andrew to clean his boots. When the youth refused, the Captain raised his saber to strike him across the head with the blunt edge of the weapon. Andrew threw up his arm to parry the blow, causing the sword to glance across his forehead, leaving a scar.

Andrew and Robert Jackson were then taken to a British prison in Camden, South Carolina, where an epidemic of smallpox broke out. Robert contracted the disease and died, but Andrew was released thanks to the tearful entreaties of his mother.

Within a year, Andrew's mother also died of smallpox, so at the age of 14, he was thrown on his own. He was bitter through and through. Because of the British, he had lost his mother and two brothers. The scar he carried on his forehead reminded him of this fact, and he swore to get his revenge. He got his chance on January 8, 1815.

In a postscript to the War of 1812, Andrew Jackson was commanding a hodgepodge of 7000 militia. He was facing 8000 crack British troops near New Orleans. No one would have blamed him if he had retreated up the Natchez Trace, but Jackson was not one to retreat from anyone—especially the English. As the confident enemy approached, Jackson traced the scar in his forehead with his fingers, and his anger rekindled anew.

When the day was over, Jackson had his revenge, for you see, 2000 British soldiers lay dead or wounded before him. By comparison, there were only 70 American causalities. Although it took over 30 years, in a satisfying twist in time, Jackson got his revenge. That British officer who scarred Andrew back in the Waxhaws probably did as much to win the Battle of New Orleans as anyone who fought there on that day.

HOW THE AMERICAN REVOLUTION BROKE FAMILY BONDS

William Franklin

It is a well-known fact that the Civil War tore at the very fabric of America's family life. In that conflict, when brother fought against brother and father against son, many of the filial bonds that had held society together were cut. The War Between the States, however, was not the only struggle that put a strain on family ties. The American Revolution operated every bit as effectively to sever family affiliations. Take for instance that situation in New Jersey between the Royal Governor and his famous father.

In 1776, as the inexorable tide of revolution rolled through the American colonies, the Governor of New Jersey found himself dangerously out of step with his fellow citizens. Although born in America, he had spent much of his life in England where he had earned a Master's degree at Oxford and was later accepted to the bar. In 1763, at the conclusion of the French and Indian War, he came back home to be named royal governor of New Jersey.

The first two years of his term were pleasant and uneventful, and he was instrumental in founding Queens College, now known as Rutgers University. In 1765, however, he was unable to enforce the Stamp Act passed by Parliament, and when the spirit of revolution began to build, he was powerless stop it, even if he had wanted to do so.

Clearly independence was in the air, but the Governor couldn't bring himself to surrender his loyalty to King George, notwithstanding the fact that his father, who would soon sign the Declaration of Independence, implored his son to embrace the Patriot cause. The son held firm and soon found himself in trouble.

With relations between the Mother Country and the colonies already shattered by fighting, New Jersey's governor was placed under house arrest in January 1776, and in June he was taken to Connecticut and held as a prisoner of war for the next two and a half years. Later he was officially stripped of his office by the provincial legislature, and exiled to England, which was something akin to throwing the rabbit into the briar patch. Meanwhile, the Governor's father continued his fight against the British.

The son never came back to America, and he never really reconciled with his father, who a few years before his death finally broke down and wrote his wayward son a letter. "Nothing has ever hurt me…, as to find myself deserted in my old age by my only son; and not only deserted, but to find him taking up arms against me in a cause wherein my good fame, fortune, and life were all at stake."

You see, that son who spurned his father's counsel and turned his back on the patriot cause was none other than William Franklin, the son of Benjamin Franklin. In a tragic twist in time, father and son were separated by the schism that created the United States of America, and the son was on the losing side.

BENJAMIN FRANKLIN'S THANKSGIVING LEGACY

American Eagle vs Franklin's Turkey

The first American Thanksgiving was celebrated in 1621, to commemorate the harvest reaped by the Pilgrims after a disastrous winter. In the years that followed, Americans institutionalized the Plymouth Colony observance, and as a result, the turkey has emerged to symbolize what is now a national holiday of Thanksgiving. If Benjamin Franklin had had his way, however, the bird would have ended up being saluted instead of being stuffed and eaten.

On July 4, 1776, just after the adoption of the Declaration of Independence, the Second Continental Congress appointed a committee made up of Thomas Jefferson, John Adams, and Benjamin Franklin to design an official national seal. It took six years to come up with an idea that appealed to Congress. In a split decision, they chose the American bald eagle, which brought forth a caustic assessment from Franklin, the dissenter.

The nation's elder statesman immediately opposed the choice. Franklin declared that the eagle was "a bird of bad moral character; he does not get his living honestly."

He went on to charge that the eagle can be seen more often than not "perched in some dead tree where, too lazy to fish for himself, he watches the labor of a fishing hawk… pursues him and takes the fish."

In addition to his dishonest ways, the eagle in Franklin's view was also cowardly. He pointed out that the little King Bird, "not bigger than a sparrow, attacks him boldly and drives him out of the district." In short, Benjamin Franklin bitterly opposed the adoption of the eagle as a symbol for America. He had another bird in mind.

Franklin sought to replace the eagle with a fowl that was "much more respectable and was a true original native of America." He called his choice a "bird of courage that would not hesitate to attack any Grenadier of the British Guards who should presume to invade his barn yard with a red coat on."

Fortunately for the celebration of Thanksgiving, Franklin was not successful. For you see, he wanted to replace the eagle with the turkey. If he had prevailed, one can hardly imagine Americans gathering around their dinner tables today eating their national symbol. In a fateful twist in time, Franklin lost the argument but in the long run made possible the elevated status the turkey has today on America's dinner tables. One has to wonder how the turkeys feel about this.

THE MARYLAND PARSON AND HIS LITTLE WHITE LIE

Parson Weems Fable

    The parish priest probably lived 100 years before his time. Born in 1760, this preacher with a penchant for exaggeration was endowed with superb oratorical skills and a thirst for flamboyancy, which could have rivaled P.T. Barnum a century later. As it was, he had to content himself with entertaining his parishioners and spinning spellbinding yarns for a grateful nation that was in search of a hero.

    Oddly enough, the ministry was not his first choice among professions. When the Peace of Paris ended the Revolutionary War in 1783, he left his Maryland farm and his 18 siblings to study medicine, but it didn't require a great deal of time for him to turn to theology. There was something restrictive about treating one patient at a time. He much preferred a whole roomful.

    As a member of the Church of England, which became the Episcopal Church in America, the young, would-be clergyman traveled to London in 1784, for ordination. Upon his return to the United States, the newly designated man of God set about preaching with a passion to several congregations in his native Maryland. Using a fiery style that appealed to the emotions, this shepherd of the flock both instructed and entertained folks for eight or nine years. Then he stumbled onto his real calling.

Not wholly satisfied with life in the pulpit, he began to toy with printing and selling religious works. That is how he met pioneer publisher, Matthew Carey, who convinced him to turn in his collar and become a bookseller.

The Parson reveled in his new trade as a traveling salesman, and in time he began to write himself. At first he produced a series of "improvement books," that dealt with marriage, dueling, gambling and adultery. By the late 1790s his work had attracted a large following. Then in 1799, he really stepped onto the stage of history!

George Washington died in that year, and the nation went into deep mourning. That's when the Parson decided to seize the day. He sat down and comforted the country by writing the President's biography, and as a result, children to this day are often taught that our first chief executive could never tell a lie.

For you see, this literary Parson was none other than Mason Locke Weems, the man who wrote, <u>The Life of George Washington</u>, which contained that story about the chopping down of the cherry tree.

In an opportune twist in time, Parson Weems used the President's death to write his largely fictitious and lavishly embellished account of Washington's life, and for years thereafter school children across the land were taught to idolize the man. In the meantime, Parson Weems discovered that writing could be very lucrative as long as it was interesting. His stories about George Washington didn't have to be true; they just had to be good.

THE BROUHAHA OVER THE BONES OF DANIEL BOONE

The name of Daniel Boone is synonymous with the Westward Movement. He is remembered as the buckskin frontiersman who opened up Kentucky for pioneer settlement. He fought Indians, explored the wilderness, and built a fort that he named Boonsborough. In the process, he became one of America's folk heroes. So revered was Daniel Boone that 25 years after he died, folks in Frankfort, Kentucky, followed his trail to Missouri to exhume his body, never dreaming that they were about to make a terrible mistake.

After he had explored Kentucky, Daniel Boone remained there until 1795, when an influx of settlers sent him scurrying for a new frontier. He found it in Missouri. Daniel took his wife, Rebecca, and their son, Nathan, and settled on Femme Osage Creek. Later they moved to Marthasville.

Daniel Boone

On March 18, 1813, Rebecca Boone died, and they buried her in Marthasville. Later, Daniel, now an old man, went to live with his son in Defiance, Missouri, some 14 miles away. On September 26, 1820, at the age of 86, the famed frontiersman passed away. He remains were then interred near his wife's grave at Marthasville, and there they both remained until September 13, 1845, when a commission from Frankfort, Kentucky, exhumed the bones of both Rebecca and Daniel, and that's how the brouhaha began.

On the day the Boone bones were brought to Frankfort for reburial, the city went into a frenzy. People came from all over Kentucky to watch the mile-long procession make its way to the cemetery. The hearse was decorated with evergreens and flowers and drawn by four white horses. Once they reached the graveyard, the townspeople performed a funeral service with the Honorable John J. Crittenden presiding. Then the two coffins were lowered into the ground. One contained the body of Rebecca Boone, and the other held the final remains of Daniel Boone, or at least that is what everyone thought.

The ceremony at Frankfort, however, was no sooner over, than tales began to emanate across the state line from Defiance, Missouri. Rumors had it that, while the Frankfort delegation had indeed recovered Rebecca's bones, Daniel's remained precisely where they had been deposited 25 years earlier. The folks at Defiance claimed that when he died, Daniel had been buried at his wife's feet because the space next to Rebecca was occupied with another body.

In 1845, the Frankfort folks, thinking that Daniel would be at Rebecca's side, dug up the wrong person. With glee, the citizens of Defiance spread the story of the dilemma of Boone's bones.

The Frankfort people of course denied the claims of the folks from Missouri, and over the years the controversy grew. Finally in 1983, the body that had been buried next to Rebecca Boone in Frankfort was exhumed once again, and a forensic anthropologist made a plastic cast of the skull and studied it. His conclusion made jaws drop all over Kentucky.

The scientist had determined that the people of Defiance, Missouri were right after all, for you see, the body that had been exhumed in Missouri and brought to Frankfort for reburial was not Daniel Boone's. It was that of a large African-American. In an unusual twist in time, Daniel Boone was accidentally left in Missouri, while his wife and the body of a stranger were taken to Kentucky.

At first blush, it would seem that an injustice has been done, until one contemplates what sent Boone to Missouri in the first place. He went there to avoid the crowds. One is forced to ask, then, whether he would not prefer his lonely resting-place in Missouri as opposed to a spot in a crowded cemetery in Frankfort, Kentucky. One suspects that he would.

BOYS GO WILD AT HARVARD

Charles Adams

The days should have been happy ones for John Adams. After ten years overseas in the diplomatic service of the newly created United States, he was finally back home. He had just been elected to the office of Vice President under the recently adopted Constitution, and his wife, Abigail, was preparing to join him in the nation's first capital, New York City.

These blessings notwithstanding, however, this was a bleak time for Adams. Not only were his countrymen suddenly turning against him, one of his sons had brought shame on the family name through some unthinkable antics in college.

From the time that he was escorted to the dais from which as Vice President he would preside over the United States Senate, unexpected pressure and criticism buffeted Adams. The first order of business was to decide how to address President George Washington. Some senators preferred to simply refer to him as "Mr. President," while others sought to honor him with something more dignified like, "Excellency." As for John Adams, he preferred "His Highness the President of the United States and Protector of the Rights of the Same." This of course got him into big trouble with the representatives of the common man who loathed anything that resembled sympathy for the forms of monarchy.

Of course the stubborn Adams would not relent or compromise without a lengthy fight. The debate went on for over a month, and during that time, the Vice President was publicly castigated for his position. As much as this criticism mortified Adams, however, it paled by comparison when he got word of his son's trouble at Harvard.

Everyone knew that Charles Adams was possessed of a flighty spirit. As a teenage student at Harvard, he exhibited a frivolity that worried his father, and in the summer of 1789, this concern proved to be well placed. Right in the midst of the turmoil of his first few weeks as Vice President, John Adams had to deal with another crisis—this one within his own family. As if his political problems weren't enough, Adams was embarrassed to tears by Charles' conduct, which had forced him out of Harvard and landed him in New York where his father could deal with him.

You see, Charles had fallen into bad company at Harvard, and contrary to the accepted norms for student behavior, he and some friends went on a drinking binge one night and committed the unpardonable. They took off their clothes and ran naked through Harvard Yard! In a hilarious twist in time, Charles Adams and his colleagues performed the first recorded act of "streaking" on a college campus in the United States.

It didn't take John Adams long to parry those political darts that had been thrown at him during his first days as Vice President, but the shocking behavior of his son on the hallowed grounds of Harvard continued to plague him for months to come.

After all, what was a Puritan to do with a son whose sense of propriety was formed centuries ahead of his time?

GONE BUT NOT FORGOTTEN

John Quincy Adams

Lieutenant William Barron loved his native Virginia, but he loved the sea even more. By the time of the American Revolution, he had sailed all over the world, and he brought that experience to bear when he joined the infant navy of Great Britain's rebellious colonies. Unfortunately, Barron's service was cut short by a tragic accident, and he was buried at sea, with the help of a ten-year-old passenger who was destined to leave his own imprint on the pages of American history.

William Barron's farewell voyage began on February 17, 1778, aboard the *Boston* a 114-foot frigate, which was sailing from Marblehead, Massachusetts, to Bordeaux, France. Since winter crossings of the Atlantic were always hazardous at best, everyone aboard was prepared for the worst, but none could have foreseen the bizarre episode that would take place on March 19, especially that little ten-year-old passenger.

The young Boston lad, who was traveling with his father, had drawn close to Lieutenant Barron, not only because he was the ship's first mate, but also because he took time to show the youngster the ways of the sea. In fact, the boy quickly became something of an apprentice seaman to Lieutenant Barron by the time the *Boston* passed the Azores.

On that fateful March morning, while Barron had the watch, he spotted a French brig sailing west. The ship's captain ordered him to prepare a signal shot, but when the gun was fired, it blew to pieces, felling several sailors and shattering Lieutenant Barron's leg. The first mate's horrified young passenger friend ran across the deck in tears. He rightly feared for the life of his newly found mentor.

The ship's surgeon amputated Barron's mangled leg, but it was not enough to save the life of the injured man. Within a week he was dead.

On March 26, 1778, as the *Boston* ran parallel to the French coast, its crew prepared Lieutenant William Barron for burial. They put his body in a chest and then dumped 10 or 12 pounds of shot in with him. After the makeshift coffin was nailed shut, the fragments of the gun that had exploded were lashed on top, and the whole was carried to the side of the ship.

At that point, the deceased's young friend, the 10-year-old who had been at his side since they had weighed anchor off the Massachusetts coast, was invited to assist in the sea burial. He helped slide the chest overboard and then stepped back to watch his hero's body sink to its watery grave.

Thus did Lieutenant William Barron depart this world, but he was not forgotten. For you see, that precocious little 10-year-old who idolized him was none other than John Quincy Adams, who was destined to become the sixth President of the United States. Through a strange twist in time, in the years that followed, Adams kept alive the memory of his friend every time he recalled that first trip across the Atlantic in which he was literally shown the ropes by a thoughtful old man of the sea.

THE PERSONIFICATION OF AMERICA

Uncle Sam

At first blush, Mr. Wilson didn't appear to be anything out of the ordinary. He was a typical 18th century American who supported his family and proved his patriotism by going off to war. By the time that he died, however, his name had become a household word, thanks to his admiring nephews.

Wilson was born in 1766, in Massachusetts. In 1781, at the age of 15, he enlisted to fight the British in the Revolutionary War. After the colonies won their independence, he and his brother, Ebenezer, set out for Troy, New York, to find their fortune.

It was in Troy that Wilson met and married Betsy Mann, who had a dozen nephews, all of whom took a liking to their new, easy-going uncle. Not long after his marriage, Wilson started a meat packing business in which he employed many of those nephews. This of course further endeared their uncle to them.

Then the War of 1812 hit. Although he was too old to fight in America's Second War for Independence, Wilson nevertheless did his part. He signed a contract to supply beef and pork to the War Department. The Troy meat packer worked day and night stuffing his provisions into barrels and then sending them to the soldiers. Their uncle's indefatigable fortitude did not go unnoticed by that bevy of nephews whom he had put to work, and they set about to perpetuate his place in history by stamping special brands on his meat barrels.

With every cask of meat that left Wilson's premises, his nephews saw to it that each was clearly marked. Soon everyone recognized the barrels, and Mr. Wilson's fame began to spread. By the time of his death on July 31, 1854, Wilson's loyal nephews had built their uncle into a regional icon. It didn't take long for Wilson then to become a national figure.

Thomas Nast, the 19th century cartoonist, added to Wilson's reputation by including drawings of him in his publications. Then in 1961, Congress saluted Mr. Wilson and his reputation by declaring him to be the official personification of the United States, complete with a white goatee and a star-spangled suit.

For you see, Mr. Wilson's first name was Sam, and those markings made by his nephews on his meat barrels were the letters "U" and "S." At first people took them to stand for the United States, but before long they stood for both the man—Uncle Sam—and his country.

Now through a nostalgic twist in time, Mr. Wilson lies in sweet repose in Troy, New York, and over him is a fitting marker to remind Americans that there once was a real, live Uncle Sam and that behind every folk legend there is always a little truth.

THE AMERICAN IDOL WHO DIDN'T TELL EVERYTHING HE KNEW

George Washington

In the 1750s, the inhabitants of the royal colony of Virginia cast wary eyes over the Blue Ridge and Allegheny Mountains to the Ohio Country. A rival European power, France, could be seen encroaching on what the royal governor, Robert Dinwiddie, considered to be Virginia's territory, so he sent a detachment of troops under the command of a twenty-two year old Lieutenant Colonel to harry the intruders out of the land. As a result, the first shots of the French and Indian War were fired, and the young officer presided helplessly over a scene of butchery that he later tried hard to hide.

On May 28, 1754, the Virginians, who were allied with an Indian band led by Chief Tanacharison, came upon thirty-two French soldiers encamped in a forest glen. The Frenchmen, after an initial exchange of gunfire, threw down their weapons and tried to surrender. Their leader, Monsieur De Jumonville, tried to explain that they had come to negotiate, not fight. While he was talking, Tanacharison slipped up behind him and struck him in the head with a hatchet, splitting his skull. The Chief's followers took that as a sign to exact the proverbial pound of flesh from their enemies.

The Indians fell on the wounded French soldiers and scalped them all, after which they decapitated one and stuck his head on a stake. Then came the highpoint of the carnage. Chief Tanacharison walked over to Jumonville's body and pried his skull apart. He then pulled out the Frenchman's brain and washed his hands in the mixture of blood and tissue. All the while the stunned young Virginian in charge sat helplessly on his horse and did nothing.

When the rampage was over and the youthful commander wrote out his report, he hid the real horror of the encounter by making it as antiseptic as possible. "…we killed 10, wounded one and took 21 prisoners," he wrote. "Amongst those that were killed was Monsieur De Jumonville." There was no mention of the atrocities committed by his Indian allies.

In a letter to his brother, the Colonel glossed over the killings by focusing on his own sense of danger. "I heard bullets whistle, and believe me, there was something charming in the sound."

Not even in his diary could the militiaman be forthright. He tried to convince himself that Jumonville's claim that he was on a diplomatic mission was all pretence.

It was of course impossible to conceal the truth of the massacre forever. When the Virginians returned home, the story leaked out in bits and pieces, but the young commander always downplayed the atrocity. He never shouldered any responsibility for the bloodbath, especially after the people put him on a pedestal. For you see, the youthful leader of that fateful expedition was none other than George Washington, the Father of Our Country.

In a fateful twist in time, it seems that the man, who was thought to have been unable to tell a lie, had no trouble in hiding the truth.

THE FOUNDING FATHER WITH A WANDERING EYE

Abigail Adams

History remembers James Lovell as a diehard patriot. He went to prison for his anti-British views and later became a member of the Continental Congress, representing Massachusetts. Upon his arrival in Philadelphia, his fellow delegates chose him to serve on the Committee for Foreign Affairs. It would have been more appropriate, however, if they had created a spot for him on the Committee for Domestic Affairs, or better yet, chairman of the Committee for Affairs of the Heart, for this is the arena in which one of America's most cunning Founding Fathers excelled.

    Lovell had no sooner taken his seat on the Foreign Affairs Committee than he led the movement to send fellow Massachusetts delegate John Adams to France in search of an ally in the struggle with Great Britain. James contended that his friend's presence in Paris was all that was needed to bring Louis XVI on the side of the colonists. "We want a man of inflexible integrity," wrote Lovell.

Although it took some coaxing, Adams finally agreed, and on February 17, 1778, he said goodbye to his wife, Abigail, and set sail for France. Lovell, meanwhile, was left free to pursue his nefarious plot. He would do his best to make sure that Mrs. Adams did not suffer from loneliness.

In his first letter to Abigail, James attempted to get his foot in the door by extolling John's virtues as a husband and patriot. Abigail wrote back, "This is a painful situation, and my patience is nearly exhausted." A delighted Lovell now saw his chance.

More letters followed, and in one Lovell, by insinuation, planted a doubt about John's fidelity. He wrote that she must not imagine her husband doing anything in his private hours in Paris other than attending museums. This must have raised suspicions in Abigail's mind, for in a letter to his wife, Adams wondered, from the tone of her letters, "If some 'infernal' might be whispering insinuations in her ear." He wasn't far from the truth.

In the months that followed, Lovell became more and more transparent in his intentions until finally he wrote, "If ye were mine… how dearly I would love thee." He underscored the word love. A weakening Abigail answered that he was "a most ingenious and agreeable flatterer," and signed the letter "Portia," her husband's pet name for her.

Finally though, after eleven months of correspondence, Lovell went too far, too fast by injecting an outrageous double entendre that restored Abigail to her Puritan moorings. You see, when he expressed relief that her husband's "rigid patriotism" (again underscored) had not left her pregnant again," Abigail called a screeching halt to their flirtatious exchanges by writing, "I begin to look upon you as a very dangerous man." In a redeeming twist in time, Mrs. Adams came to her senses. She could not abide such blatantly suggestive images, not even from one of America's Founding Fathers.

SEGREGATION ASSAULTED IN EARLY AMERICA

It is a well-known fact that Booker T. Washington had a powerful influence on President Theodore Roosevelt. The former slave was sought out many times for advice by the "Rough Rider." In fact in 1901, Washington visited Roosevelt in the White House, and after their meeting, the two had dinner. This raised eyebrows all over the country, since folks were under the impression that a black man had never before dined with a United States President in the presidential living quarters.

As a matter of fact, however, Booker T. Washington was not the first black leader to cross the color line at a presidential lunch counter. That barrier was broken in 1799 in Philadelphia.

It all happened after the black inhabitants of San Domingo (Haiti) rose up against their French masters in 1791. It was a bloody revolt that lasted for years and was led by one Toussaint L'Ouverture, who by 1799 was desperate for food for his starving troops.

Toussaint L'Ouverture

BILL COATE

As fate would have it, the United States had its own quarrel with France at the time. War fever was running rampant as the French Navy conducted an undeclared war on American shipping. In retaliation, the United States issued a trading embargo against France and its colonies, which of course included San Domingo.

Thus it was that L'Ouverture felt optimistic in appealing to President John Adams for succor. He wanted two things. First he wrote asking that the Congress repeal that part of the embargo that applied to San Domingo. Second, and most important, the Haitian leader asked that the United States extend recognition to his insurgent government. Adams signaled his interest, and that is how Joseph Bunel, Toussaint's representative, came to be in Philadelphia in 1799.

In a meeting with the President, Bunel insisted that American ships would be welcomed and protected in San Domingo. It was agreed that Commodore John Barry would take two heavy frigates *United States* and *Constitution* to Cape Francois in a show of support for L'Ouverture. In addition, Bunel convinced Adams not only to lift the embargo, but also to give de facto recognition to the Caribbean island.

For Bunel, the negotiations were a clean sweep. He got everything he wanted, and the President presented Congress with Bunel's wish list, which carried the curious name of "Toussaint's Clause."

With their diplomatic work complete, Adams invited his guest to join him in making history, for you see, the two dined together that night in Adams' residence. In an egalitarian twist in time, Joseph Bunel became the first person of African descent to be the dinner guest of an American President. It would be another 100 years before such an event would occur again, but like Roger Bannister and the four-minute mile, the barrier, once breached, was destined to give way for ever.

BLACKMAIL, BRIBERY, AND THE PRESIDENT

President Thomas Jefferson

Thomas Jefferson, the third President of the United States, has been generally embraced by American History as a demi-god and one of our founding fathers. There is one area of his life, however, that has drawn considerable scrutiny. Rumors have been afloat for over 200 years that he had a long-standing affair with one of his slaves, Sally Hemings. As to the truth of the allegation, no one knows for sure, but one thing is certain. When the story broke in 1802, President Jefferson unsuccessfully tried to hush it up. If only he had put forth just a little more effort, he might not have a stain on his reputation today.

The culprit who was responsible for impugning Jefferson was James Callender, a former political ally. During the latter part of John Adams' term as our second Federalist President, Callender, in concert with the political opposition, which included Jefferson, excoriated the President in public. This act of vile partisanship won James a term in prison under the Alien and Sedition Acts and a burdensome fine.

By 1801, Callender was out of prison, but he still had the fine to pay, so he decided to make an appeal to what he thought would be a sure source of help—Thomas Jefferson, who was by now the President of the United States.

Callender felt that Jefferson owed him a lot; therefore, he was not at all bashful about asking for assistance. The President responded with the offer of a job—postmaster in Richmond, which Callender peremptorily dismissed as woefully inadequate. He packed his bags and headed for Washington to see Secretary of State, James Madison.

During his meeting with Madison, Callender explained that he thought Jefferson owed him much, much more. James pointed out that he had done Jefferson's dirty work for him by publicly criticizing President Adams and had paid the price for his service. Now it was Jefferson's turn to be loyal, and to insure this, Callender whispered in Madison's ear that he had some dirt on Jefferson that would be most embarrassing if ever it were leaked. James assured Madison that if the President weren't more helpful, the threatened revelation would surely come to pass.

When Madison shared Callender's threat with Jefferson, the shocked President called his secretary, Meriwether Lewis, into the room and ordered him to send his former ally some money. It was, however, to no avail. When Callender received his hush money, he was insulted. You see, Jefferson had sent him $50 to keep him quiet. Sadly for the President, the amount hardly satisfied the needs of his nemesis.

In a traitorous twist in time, James Callender then went

to the press with his allegation that President Thomas Jefferson was keeping a domestic slave in Monticello as his concubine, and that's how the cat was let out of the bag—a cat that is still running around to this very day.

For his part, Thomas Jefferson neither confirmed nor denied Callender's allegation, and the rumor went forth throughout the land all because the President's bribe didn't satisfy the demands of his blackmailer.

BEN'S BOOZE
DID THE TRICK

Ben Franklin

Benjamin Franklin was indeed a giant among America's founding fathers. Every school child knows of his scientific curiosity, his diplomatic skills, and his journalistic prowess. They also know of Franklin's huge storehouse of common sense. Who hasn't heard the aphorism, "Early to bed and early to rise makes a man healthy, wealthy, and wise?" Indeed, readers the world over know of Franklin's wit and wisdom, but few have ever heard of his guile and how one time he tricked a company of soldiers into attending religious services during the French and Indian War.

The year was 1756, and the French had defeated British General Braddock and sent George Washington scampering home after having two horses shot out from under him and four bullet holes put in his coat.

To counter the French threat in the Ohio River Valley, the Pennsylvania Assembly commissioned Benjamin Franklin as a colonel of the militia and placed him in charge of 500 men. His job was to construct a series of defensive forts along the Ohio River.

At first things went quite well for Franklin. He had a peaceful camp at Lehigh Gap and enjoyed dining on the ample provisions his wife, Deborah, had sent with him. In time, however, trouble raised its ugly head, and it didn't have a French uniform. The difficulty lay with Franklin's chaplain. He couldn't convince the rowdy frontiersmen to attend Sunday's worship service.

Colonel Franklin, although he had no strong feelings one way or the other about the divine services, thought it best to maintain discipline within the ranks, so he ordered the troops to go to church. Alas, not even the likes of Benjamin Franklin could convince the militiamen to tend to matters spiritual on the Lord's Day. It would take more than a lightening rod to make the men listen to a Sunday sermon, so the Colonel dipped deeply into his haversack of ideas and came up with a sure-fire winner.

The next Sunday, every man in Franklin's contingent showed up for worship. Each man dutifully partook of his share of the service. Commenting on the sudden turn of events, Ben recorded in his diary, "Never were prayers more generally and punctually attended." And to what explanation did Franklin lay this change in military behavior? Booze, of all things!

You see, when he found out that it was going to take a great movement of the Spirit to move the men to worship, Franklin turned to spirits. In a guileful twist in time, Franklin assigned to the militia's chaplain the task of doling out the daily allowance of rum, and on Sundays, he ordered him to withhold the libation until just *after* worship.

Thus it was that, with the chaplain in charge of the keg and the timing of the distribution of its contents, observance of divine services never suffered again—thanks to the ingenuity of Benjamin Franklin, the willingness of the clergyman, and the thirst of the soldiers.

Presidential Oddities
With A Twist

DID WASHINGTON TELL THE TRUTH ABOUT HIS AGE?

George Washington

The celebration of George Washington's birthday is almost as old as the nation itself. It was first publicly observed before he left office, and after he died, the commemorations proliferated. This national recognition of Washington's birthday continued to gain momentum over the years until Congress acted in 1885, to make February 22nd a national holiday, but therein lay a problem.

In signing the holiday legislation, President Chester Arthur enshrined that day. Schools across the nation held Washington Day pageants in honor of the first President. Teachers made their students memorize February 22, 1732, and explain its significance. Paeans of praise poured forth in the columns of the newspapers, and February 22nd became a red-letter day for all Americans. Little did they know just how little they knew.

For the next 83 years Americans continued to recognize February 22, 1732, as George Washington's birthday. Then in 1968, Congress passed the Monday Holidays Act, which moved the official observance of Washington's birthday from February 22nd to the third Monday in February. Although most workers got a three-day weekend, February 22nd was still a highly revered day because that was the actual day our first President was born, or at least that was what the people had been told.

Today the third Monday in February is known as Presidents' Day due to an effort by Richard Nixon in 1971, to include the memory of Abraham Lincoln along side that of Washington. In actuality, Nixon's effort notwithstanding, the day remains officially a federal holiday in honor of George Washington because Congress neither intended nor authorized the inclusion of Lincoln or any other President in the Monday Holidays Act.

It is not unexpected then that a little confusion reigns during February of each year. On the third Monday of the month, some folks honor all of the Presidents. Others honor only Washington and Lincoln, and some honor just Washington. All the while, a few purists hold fast to February 22nd as the day to pay their respects.

In reality, however, it doesn't make any difference, as far as Washington is concerned. For you see, February 22nd was not his birthday, and he was not born in 1732!

At the time of Washington's birth, Great Britain and her colonies were living under the Julian calendar, which had come down from Roman times. According to that system of dating, the English New Year fell on March 25th, the Feast of the Annunciation. Thus, Washington, having been born on February 11th had a birth year of 1731.

Then in 1752, Britain adopted the more accurate Gregorian calendar, which shifted the start of the New Year to January 1st, and Washington's birthday to February 22, 1732. And there it remains to this day. In a confusing twist in time, the British Empire gave George Washington a new birthday. One has to wonder how long it took him to determine precisely how old he was.

WASHINGTON'S FINAL SECRET

Martha Washington

Some say that the measure of a man is how he dies. If that is true, the father of our country, George Washington, stands tall among men. He held his composure right to the end, as he calmly accepted the fact that he was about to leave this world. Just before he died however, he did something, which apparently caused him no concern, but left an unsettled feeling among those he left behind.

Washington's demise began without warning on the morning of December 13, 1799. He was laying plans for some improvements to the front of Mount Vernon and was outside taking measurements. When the rain and sleet came, he had just a bit more to do, so he continued. As a result, when he came inside he was soaked.

About one o'clock in the afternoon chills and nausea seized him. By suppertime, he was worse, so Martha Washington chided him for working when he was sick and put him to bed.

All night long, Washington tossed and turned with a fever and pain. By morning, it was agreed that a physician should be called. Couriers were dispatched to Dr. Craik, the family doctor, along with Drs. Dick and Brown, the consulting physicians. They were all prompt with their responses.

As the night of December 14 approached, Washington got worse. From his bed he told Dr. Craik, "I am dying, sir-- but am not afraid to die." Then he called his wife Martha to his side. He instructed her "Go to my desk, and in the private drawer you will find two papers. Bring them to me."

Martha did as she was told, and while she was gone, Washington gave instructions for his funeral. Then with amazing self-possession, he folded his arms across his chest and waited for Martha's return.

When she reentered the room with the two papers, Washington called her to him and whispered in her ear, "These are my Wills. Preserve this one and burn the other."

She immediately left the room with both papers and in a few moments returned with just one. No one but Martha Washington knew the contents of the copy that was burned— not even her husband, for you see, Mrs. Washington had left the room alone. Only she knew which Will was actually burned. Her husband never saw the one with which she returned.

And what were the provisions of Washington's Will? In an unusual twist in time, instead of only the usual widow's portion, Mrs. Washington received possession of virtually all of her husband's possessions during her lifetime and the beneficiary of the profits derived from them.

One has to wonder what was in the other Will—the one nobody but Martha saw.

THE SCOUNDREL WHO ALMOST BECAME PRESIDENT

Aaron Burr

Aaron Burr was really a scoundrel of a man. He murdered Alexander Hamilton in a duel he knew he would win; he tried to lead a rebellion against the United States, and most importantly, he tried to steal the election of 1800. Had it not been for one conscientious congressman from Delaware, in this last instance, Burr might have been successful.

BILL COATE

In the fall of 1800, John Adams and his Federalist Party prepared for a second run for the Presidency. Opposing Adams was his own Vice President, Thomas Jefferson, who had formed a new party appropriately named the Jeffersonian Republicans. The Federalists chose Charles Pinckney to run with Adams while the Republicans picked Aaron Burr to fill their second spot.

The actual voting took place on December 3 in the state capitals of the 16 states that made up the United States at the time. When the tally was counted, the people were in for a shock. It was a tie but not between Jefferson and Adams. Rather, it was Jefferson and his running mate, Aaron Burr who garnered the same number of votes.

In those days before the 12th Amendment, each elector simply voted for two men, without specifying for which office he was casting his vote—the President or the Vice President. In an unfortunate show of political solidarity, the Republicans held to the party line, and cast 73 votes for both Jefferson and Burr. Thus the election was thrown into the House of Representatives where each state delegation was given one vote.

Everybody expected Burr to urge the congressmen to vote for Jefferson, since he, Burr, had been the clear choice of the party to become the Vice President. They reckoned, however, without the cunning of Burr. The New Yorker saw an unexpected opportunity, so he kept quiet and just watched. On February 11, 1801, the first roll call was taken. It took the votes of nine state delegations to win, and on that first round Jefferson, with eight, fell one short. Burr garnered 6 votes, while two states were hopelessly deadlocked.

For six gut-wrenching days, the House of Representatives tried to elect a new President, and each time the result was the same. Eight state delegations voted for Jefferson, and six voted for Burr. The Maryland and Vermont delegations remained deadlocked and could not be counted, leaving Jefferson one vote shy of the necessary nine votes.

Back and forth the voting went, while appeals to Burr to release his support fell on deaf ears. The future Vice President wasn't about to allow this unexpected opportunity to slip through his fingers. That's when James Bayard decided to save the country from a constitutional crisis.

You see, as Delaware's only congressman, Bayard had complete control of his state's vote, thus he was able to settle the election. On the 36th roll call, he switched Delaware from the Burr column to Jefferson, giving him the required nine votes and the Presidency. In a fateful twist in time, Aaron Burr had to settle for the Vice Presidency, and it is a good thing. Who could have imagined the political fallout if Burr had been President when he killed Alexander Hamilton and had to run the ship of state while eluding those authorities who wanted to arrest him for murder?

JOHN QUINCY ADAMS IS CAUGHT IN A COMPROMISING POSITION

President John Quincy Adams

Anne Royall was a female with whom very few wished to trifle. Born in Baltimore in 1769, she was destined to teach America the much needed lesson that there were some women who would stand up for their rights, even if it meant sneaking up on the President of the United States while he was skinny-dipping.

Anne was 28 years old when she married Major William Royall, a Revolutionary War veteran. In 1812, she became a wealthy widow when the Major died, leaving her fixed for life, or so she thought.

Much to Anne's chagrin, however, several of Major Royall's male relatives quickly challenged his will. The matter wound up in court, where Anne didn't stand a chance. The litigation continued for seven years, and finally the document was declared a forgery. Anne Royall was left penniless to fend for herself in a man's world. She proved equal to the task.

After her defeat in court, Anne traveled to Washington D.C. to petition for a pension as the widow of a Revolutionary War soldier. She started with Secretary of State, John Quincy Adams. He agreed that the pension program needed reform, and he consented to help her, but months melted into years, and nothing happened. Therefore, Anne decided to become the nation's first female investigative reporter and set out to expose graft and corruption in government, an effort at which she was eminently successful.

Then in 1828, she returned to the issue of her widow's pension. Somehow she discovered that John Quincy Adams, who was by now the President, went skinny-dipping every morning in the Potomac River. In those days when the President was virtually unprotected, Anne found Adams chest deep in the water with his clothes neatly folded on the bank. Sensing a rare opportunity for negotiations, Anne, sat down on the President's clothes and called out to him.

John Quincy Adams came as close to the bank as he dared, and Anne peppered him with questions about the status of her long-standing quest for a widow's pension. Adams admitted that the bureaucratic wheels had been grinding slowly, but he promised that he would give her plight his renewed attention if she would just leave so that he could get dressed. Anne complied and so did President Adams, but not right away.

It was twenty years before John Quincy Adams finally delivered on his promise. You see, after his defeat in his second run for the Presidency, he won a seat in the United States House of Representatives. Now as a member of Congress, he helped Anne secure her pension. In an ironic twist in time, it was one of the former President's last political acts. Shortly after the passage of the new pension law of 1848, Adams had a stroke on the floor of the House and died in the Speaker's office two days later.

Thus did John Quincy Adams finally keep his word to Anne Royall, the gadfly on the backs of Washington's politicians. It's just too bad he couldn't have lived a little longer. Perhaps he could have prevented her from losing her newly acquired pension to those same malcontents who had filched Anne's inheritance in the first place.

THE HIDDEN MEANING OF "HAIL TO THE CHIEF"

Sir Walter Scott

  Anyone who has ever witnessed the appearance of the President of the United States at a public event will have no difficulty recognizing the musical tribute that announces his entrance. Today we call it "Hail to the Chief," and it has been around for a long, long time. Few of us, however, know how the song ever came to be associated with Presidents or worse yet, why it was ever written at all. If we did, we would surely find some other way to honor the occupants of the White House.

  The first public performance of "Hail to the Chief" in the United States occurred in 1812, and on July 4, 1828, it was associated for the first time with an appearance of the President of the United States. The Marine Corps band played the tune when John Quincy Adams showed up on that day for the groundbreaking ceremony of the Chesapeake and Ohio Canal.

After that the song caught on, and by the time of John Tyler's administration, "Hail to the Chief" was played with some regularity at official functions. When his successor, James Knox Polk, moved into the White House, his wife, Sara Polk, made the playing of the song obligatory whenever her husband made his entrance at social events. She had grown tired of folks ignoring her short, unkempt spouse.

Over the years, "Hail to the Chief" became the unofficial notice that the President was about to make his appearance, and it remained so until the Department of Defense established it as policy in 1954. If only someone had taken the time to reflect on the background of the song, they might have chosen another one.

The words to the tune came from Sir Walter Scott's epic poem, "Lady of the Lake," and Englishman James Sanderson set them to music in the early 1800s, but they were hardly meant to instill pride in the people and their leader—quite the contrary.

The lilting melody that became "Hail to the Chief," was originally the story of the demise of a failed Scottish chieftain who had been betrayed and executed by his enemy. It laments the fickle nature of the masses with these poignant words, "Who o'er the herd would wish to reign, Fantastic, fickle, fierce, and vain?" "Thou many-headed monster-thing, O who would wish to be thy king?"

So you see, the song we play to announce the coming of the leader of the land is really the sad account of the assassination of a political leader, hardly the stuff of which confidence in the well-being of the President is made. In a macabre twist in time, we have chosen to announce the approach of our Chief Executive with the story of the tragic fall of the people's hero.

Perhaps just before every inauguration the newly elected President should be required to read Sir Walter Scott's "Lady of the Lake." He just might decide to dispense with the musical formalities of the office.

HOW DIRTY TRICKS COST ONE MAN THE PRESIDENCY

Henry Clay was a major force in American politics in the 19th century. He served in the United States Senate; he was Speaker of the House of Representatives and architect of the Compromise of 1850. Indeed, by the time of Clay's death there was only one political goal that had been denied him. He never made it to the White House, but he might have if it hadn't been for those shenanigans he pulled in 1824.

Henry Clay

The Presidential election of that year was filled with drama. Five men threw their hats into the ring for the nation's top office. John C. Calhoun from South Carolina, William H. Crawford of Georgia, Andrew Jackson of Tennessee, John Quincy Adams from Massachusetts, and Kentucky's favorite son candidate, Henry Clay, all wanted to move to Washington.

Clay's chances improved in March of 1824, when Calhoun decided to pull out and run for Vice-President, an office which he won. Then as election time drew near, Crawford had a series of paralytic strokes, which everyone assumed would prevent him from serving as President. Thus on the eve of the election, the field was, for all intents and purposes, reduced to three men: Adams, Clay, and Jackson.

When the votes were counted, Jackson came out ahead in both the popular vote (152,901) and the Electoral College (99). Adams came in second with 114, 023 of the popular votes and 84 in the Electoral College. Crawford was third with 47,217 popular votes and 41 electoral votes. Clay brought up the rear with 46,979 popular votes and 37 electoral votes. Obviously Clay would not win the prize this time around, so he got together with John Quincy Adams to lay a nefarious plan.

Since no candidate received a majority of the Electoral College votes, the election was thrown into the House of Representatives. This placed Clay, who was Speaker of the House in a most enviable position. He could swing the election.

According to the Constitution, the House would choose the President from the three highest vote getters. This left Clay out of the running, but he still had his bartering power. He sat down and made a deal—some said a corrupt bargain—with J.Q. Adams. Clay would swing the vote in the House to Adams, and the latter would appoint the former to the position of Secretary of State. Then sometime in the future, Clay expected to fulfill his life long ambition.

Naturally there were howls of protest, especially from Andrew Jackson, whom most people thought would be selected by the House. Clay, however, took it all in stride, but he didn't count on the intensity of the animosity created by his "corrupt bargain."

He ran for President again in 1832 and 1844, but never came close to winning. People didn't forget, nor did they forgive. Henry Clay burned his Presidential bridges behind him in 1824 and was never able to be more than a regional leader.

To be sure, he remained an astute and able politician right to the end, but he was never able to overcome the public perception that as far as national office was concerned he had betrayed the public trust when he helped defeat the people's choice for President in that election of 1824.

WHY ANDREW JACKSON MARRIED ANOTHER MAN'S WIFE

Andrew Jackson was as tough as nails. This is why they called him "Old Hickory." He fought duels. He fought Indians. He fought the British. He fought political enemies, and he beat them all. There were very few opponents who could survive his enmity. Then along came Lewis Robards. He made Jackson commit adultery!

Robards was the husband of Rachel Donelson, daughter of an early settler in what became Nashville, Tennessee. After three years of marriage, the insanely jealous Robards, without cause, ordered his wife out of his Kentucky home, so she returned to her family in Tennessee. That is where she met Andrew Jackson.

The young Tennessee lawyer was a family friend of the Donelson's, and as such, he saw quite a bit of the rejected Rachel. Before long a romantic spark sprang up between them, but they appropriately held it in check due to her marital status. She was still a married woman.

Although Rachel remained as pure as the driven snow and Andrew maintained his respect for the fact that she was another man's wife, rumors began to radiate out from the Donelson's home that the two were having a tête-à-tête right there on the Cumberland. It didn't take long for Robards to hear the gossip. The falsehood traveled so fast because it had so many helping hands.

Andrew Jackson continued to ride the circuit while Rachel settled in at her mother's home. He made frequent visits to the Donelson home, ostensibly to pay his respects to the entire family, but in reality to see Rachel. Before long the couple admitted to each other that they were in love, but at the same time, they resolved never to violate the law or Rachel's marriage vows by expressing that

Rachel Jackson

WWW.TwistInTime.COM

love physically. Then came that day in 1791.

Andrew Jackson came galloping up to the Donelson house on that hot August afternoon. He jumped off the horse and burst through the door without knocking. He could barely contain himself. Lewis Robards had obtained a divorce from the State Legislature. Now Andrew and Rachel were free to become man and wife, and unfortunately for their reputations, that is exactly what they did.

For two years Andrew and Rachel enjoyed extra-legal, matrimonial bliss, and then in 1793, came a bombshell. They had technically been living in adultery since August 1791, for the legislature had never granted Lewis' request for a divorce. It had all been a work of fiction. He couldn't prove his charge of desertion and adultery. Undaunted, Robards had returned home to work the situation to his advantage.

He wanted to marry a woman named Hannah Winn, but in order to do so; he had to be free of Rachel. That's why he started the rumor that he had been granted a divorce. He knew that would be all that was needed for Andrew and Rachel to illegally tie the knot and commit adultery. Once that happened, he could go back to court and make his charges stick.

Thus it was that Andrew Jackson and Rachel were thrown on the horns of a dilemma. You see they had to get married again, but by doing so, they admitted that they had been living as man and wife in an illegal arrangement.

In an ironic twist in time, Lewis Robards obtained his divorce and married Hannah Winn, while Andrew Jackson and Rachel were labeled as adulterers for the rest of their lives. In the final analysis, Lewis Robards beat Andrew without ever having to face him. The Robards affair haunted Jackson until his dying day, as he carried the burden of being the only U.S. President who was ever convicted of adultery in a court of law.

OLD HICKORY'S BARNYARD SYMBOL

Andrew Jackson

    Andrew Jackson is remembered for any number of things, but one of them is not timidity. He was never reluctant to express his political views, and he invited the nation to share his opinions with complete abandon, especially when he became President. After the common man placed Jackson in the White House in 1828, his stubbornness put such a stain on the newly organized Democratic Party that it carries his mark to this very day.

Jackson had always been a forceful personality. In his early days, with very little education, he pushed himself into becoming a judge and a member of Congress. He was the indomitable head of the Tennessee militia, and his men repaid his unwavering leadership by giving him the sobriquet, "Old Hickory."

It was after he went to Washington; however, that Jackson's certitude emerged in its most virulent form. He openly defied an edict of the United States Supreme Court and threatened to hang his former Vice-President, John C. Calhoun. He relentlessly assailed the Bank of the United States, and almost invaded the state of South Carolina because its leaders resisted his tariff policies. It was, however, the beautiful wife of his Secretary of War that caused Jackson to exhibit such uncompromising tenacity that his political enemies began to liken him to a certain barnyard animal.

Peggy O'Neal was the attractive daughter of a Washington boarding house keeper who had been linked romantically with some of her family's male guests. When Secretary of War Eaton began to court Peggy and subsequently married her, the scandal rocked the Capital. The blue-blooded wives of the rest of Jackson's cabinet entered into a compact in which they snubbed the new Mrs. Eaton. Privately, Jackson was encouraged to ask for Eaton's resignation. When the President refused, the issue went public.

The more Peggy Eaton was vilified, the more staunchly President Jackson defended her, and the more the public became involved, the more intractable Old Hickory became. The donnybrook arrived when Jackson gave his cabinet an ultimatum. They could either convince their wives to accept Mrs. Eaton, or they could resign their offices. Faced with such intransigence, only Eaton and Secretary of State, Martin Van Buren, remained.

The internal White House debate over the Eaton affair played right into the hands of Jackson's opponents in the election of 1832. They began to caricature the President and his followers in the campaign as being short on intelligence and long on a determination to have their own way, and thereby they laid the foundations for the symbol of today's Democratic Party.

For you see, the anti-Jacksonians launched a campaign to paint the President as a "jackass," and before election day the symbol of a donkey had stuck—not only on the President but on all of his followers as well, and the symbolism continues to this very day.

Through a quirky twist in time, the donkey and the Democratic Party have been merged in the public mind all because President Andrew Jackson refused to budge an inch when someone tried to take him where he didn't want to go.

THE TWO FACES
OF A WAR PROTESTER

Abraham Lincoln

In 1846, as Manifest Destiny swept the land, the United States and Mexico locked horns over Texas. That quarrel led President Polk to ask Congress for a Declaration of War. On May 13, 1846, the people's representatives responded overwhelming in the affirmative, and the fat was in the fire.

Then, in the congressional elections later that year, a gangling, rough-featured Whig from the Mid-West won a seat in the House of Representatives. He didn't play the usual political games. He wouldn't join the crowd, and he would not hold his tongue. He became a gadfly on the nose of the President over the Mexican War, and thereby earned a nickname that later followed him to the White House.

It made no difference to the Congressman that Mexico had threatened the United States with war if it annexed Texas, and he was fully aware that both sides had mobilized on the border early in 1846. His problem was that each side had its own idea as to just where to find that dividing line. Mexico said it was the Nueces River, while the United States claimed it was the Rio Grande. The Congressman wasn't sure.

He had watched from his home when on April 25, 1846, Mexican troops moved east across the Rio Grande and engaged American troops in the disputed area. He knew that sixteen U.S. soldiers had been either killed or wounded. He read the reports of an outraged President Polk who told Congress that "American blood had been spilled on American soil," and therein lay the rub for the Congressman.

When that skinny Whig with the irritating, high-pitched voice won a seat to Congress in the November elections, he rose to attack American policy in the war with Mexico. Specifically, the novice lawmaker wanted to know the precise location of the "spot" on which President Polk claimed American blood had been spilled.

The Congressman introduced resolution after resolution that requested information on exactly where the first shots were fired. Obviously he was not ready to include the disputed territory between the Rio Grande and the Nueces Rivers as "American soil." The man pushed his so-called "spot" resolutions with such persistence that he quickly acquired the nickname, "Spotty."

Unfortunately for Mexico, the rest of the United States did not go along with "Spotty." U.S. troops rolled over the Mexican army, and by 1848, they set the stage for a major land grab which included not only the disputed territory between the Rio Grande and Nueces Rivers, but California, Arizona, New Mexico, Nevada, and parts of Colorado as well.

"Spotty" never did find out to his satisfaction whether or not U.S. troops were killed on American or Mexican soil. Therefore, he was never able to justify the Mexican/American

War. He finished his one term in Congress and then went back to his home in Springfield, Illinois to fulfill his destiny.

In 1860, "Spotty" was elected President of the United States, and then he learned first hand what it was like to be a wartime President. For, as you know by now, "Spotty" was none other than Abraham Lincoln. One has to wonder what someone who did not hesitate a moment to lead his country into a war with itself in 1861, would have done if he had been President in 1846.

DID ABRAHAM LINCOLN HAVE SECOND THOUGHTS?

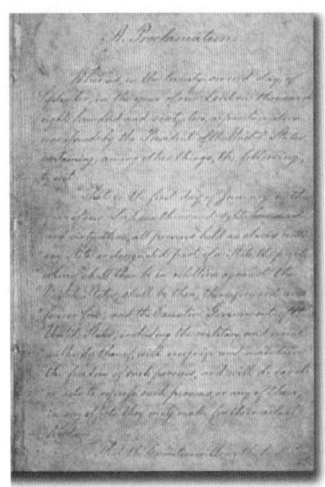

The Emancipation Proclamation

Abraham Lincoln is, of course, remembered for a great many things, and among these is the fact that he issued the Emancipation Proclamation. What is not so well known, however, is that, as much as he believed in the words of the document, he could barely force himself to sign it when the time came.

The parchment containing the Proclamation was taken to Mr. Lincoln on the afternoon of January 1, 1863. It had been announced in advance that it would be signed that day. As it lay unrolled before him, Lincoln took a pen, dipped it in ink, moved his hand to the place for the signature, held it a moment, and then removed his hand and dropped the pen. Secretary of State Seward and his son, Frederick, looked at each other, stunned.

After a moment of hesitation, Lincoln once again took up the pen and went through the same movement as before. He could not bring himself to sign the document that would declare the slaves of the Confederacy to be free. Once again, the Sewards looked at each other. Was the President having second thoughts? Secretary Seward thought as much.

This time HE picked up the pen and forced it into the hands of the President, who then began slowly to write that signature with which the entire world was so familiar, "Abraham Lincoln." When it was done, he looked up at Seward, smiled, and said simply, "That will do."

Seward then took the document to show the press corps. Within hours the telegraph wires were humming with the news, "Lincoln Proclaims Freedom for the Slaves." Meanwhile, Secretary Seward held another meeting with the President. He wanted to know why Mr. Lincoln had found it so difficult to sign the Emancipation Proclamation at the last moment. The answer was simple.

You see, he had been shaking hands since nine o'clock that morning, and his right arm was almost paralyzed. He knew that if his name ever went down in history, it would be for this act, and his whole soul is in it. If his hand had trembled when he signed the Proclamation, all who examined the document thereafter would have said, "He hesitated."

Therefore, in a strange twist in time, Abraham Lincoln appeared to have been reluctant to sign the Emancipation Proclamation. In reality, however, there were no doubts; he had simply pressed too much flesh that morning—a malaise that apparently affected politicians in his day and ours.

RECORDING HISTORY
UNDER THE PRESIDENT'S FEET

President Lincoln

Georgie Gitt was only 15 years old when he heard that the President of the United States was coming to town. The possibility of catching a glimpse of the nation's leader so thrilled the youngster that he decided to find some way to avoid the crowd that was sure to assemble. Before the day was out, Georgie got what he wanted and a whole lot more.

By the time they led the President up the wooden platform to his chair that day, Georgie was ready. He had crawled under the speakers' stand and was lying on his back looking up through the cracks in the boards.

The lad had a clear view of the President. He caught his every movement. He saw when he gazed out into space. He watched him lean from side to side as other speakers took their turn. He saw the President cross and recross his legs and rest his chin in the palm of his right hand. Georgie caught all of the body language of the President that day as he prepared to give his speech.

Before stepping to the rostrum, the President bent slightly forward and very deliberately pulled out a few flimsy pieces of paper from his coat pocket. Then he tucked them away and began to speak.

Georgie saw it all. He noted the speaker's furrowed brow and brooding eyes. He saw the handkerchief come out and wipe away the tears that trickled down his cheeks. Then came the end, and as the throngs were congratulating the President, Georgie slid out the backside of the platform and ran for the home of Judge Wills, a family friend. Georgie knew that's where they were taking the President after his speech.

Once more Georgie gained a prime spot by stealth. He entered the Wills home by the kitchen and then peeked through the door to the front hall. The Judge was just then escorting the President to the stairs. That's when Georgie made an entrance of his own.

With generosity of spirit, Judge Wills introduced Georgie Gitt and the President. They shook hands and talked for a moment, then the President started to ascend the stairs for some much-needed rest.

With a quick word of thanks, Georgie bounded out the door for his own home, and upon reaching the house, he too went for his bedroom but not to sleep. He had paper and pen all ready, and he immediately began to record his observances of that day, November 19, 1863, when he met Abraham Lincoln and heard him deliver his Gettysburg Address.

Today, not only do our National Archives have the manuscript copy of Lincoln's Gettysburg Address, but because of the determination of George D. Gitt, we also have an excellent eyewitness account of the President before, during, and after his speech. Lying on his back with eyes riveted on Lincoln, he took note of everything the President said and did that day.

Given his attentiveness to detail, it is too bad Georgie was not at Ford's Theater a few months later. He could no doubt have given the nation the 19th century equivalent of the Zapruder film.

LINCOLN
THE LEXICOGRAPHER

Mary Todd Lincoln

    Abraham Lincoln is remembered for any number of things, not the least of which is his patience with his wife, Mary Todd Lincoln. As a general rule, he was gentle to the point of being hen-pecked in the face her demanding, impervious ways. There was one time, however, in which Mary's behavior brought the President to the boiling point, and that temper tantrum had a lasting effect on the English language.

    It all happened in May of 1861. Mrs. Lincoln had gone on a shopping spree in Washington and New York, buying furniture and decorations for the White House. Unfortunately, she spent much more than the congressional budget had allocated for such items, so she began to look around for other sources to pay off the bills.

    When her husband learned of his wife's extravagance, he displayed a flush of anger, the likes of which Mary had never felt before. "It can never have my approval," he said. "I'll pay it out of my own pocket first — it would stink in the nostrils of the American people to have it said that the President of the United States had approved a bill over-running an appropriation of $20,000 for flub dubs for this damned old house, when the soldiers have nothing but "shoddy" blankets."

Now, "shoddy" was a kind of material that was used to make blankets. That material came from old woolen rags that had been torn back into fibers, soaked in oil, and then mixed with virgin wool. Normally, a blanket contained about 10% "shoddy."

Unfortunately the blanket makers got greedy and this is what had Lincoln on edge. They had increased the percentage of "shoddy" in their blankets to 25% or more. Blankets with this percentage of "shoddy" had a life of less than a month in the field, and that's what raised Lincoln's ire.

So Mary's shopping spree threw the President into a tizzy and the country began to take a good look at "shoddy" blankets. The government held investigations, and as a result, the blanket manufacturers cleaned up their act by reducing the percentage of "shoddy" they put in their products. And Mary? Well, Congress quietly passed an extra appropriation to cover her shopping spree after all. It didn't have the heart to hang the new President out to dry.

Therefore, in the end everything turned out all right. Mary Todd Lincoln refurbished the White House, and the people paid for it. The soldiers got better blankets, so the President was satisfied. The only real casualty, if indeed it can be called a casualty, was linguistic in nature.

For you see, after the President's tirade, the word "shoddy" came to denote anything of low quality, not simply a kind of material used in making wool blankets. In a unique twist in time, Abraham Lincoln changed the meaning of a word almost overnight and gave the nation one more living legacy.

HOW CIVIL PRIDE GAVE BIRTH TO MEMORIAL DAY

Abraham Lincoln's Funeral Train

Most everyone knows that Memorial Day grew out of the War Between the States. Until the advent of World War I, it was a time for folks to gather and honor the fallen soldiers of the Civil War. Later its purpose was expanded to include the soldiers who died in all of America's conflicts. In 1971, Memorial Day was made a national holiday, and Americans rejoiced over their new, three-day weekend. Ironically, however, very few knew just how it all came to be.

The seeds for Memorial Day were scattered across the country by Abraham Lincoln's funeral train. After the President's assassination, it took 14 days to carry his body back to Springfield, Illinois, for burial, and all along the way, the North reeled in an unexpected paroxysm of grief, as the rank and file rocketed Lincoln upward into sainthood.

Delirium broke out in Baltimore as cataracts of crape fell down in front of the buildings and 10,000 people shoved their way through City Hall to see the corpse. Miles out of Philadelphia, the train ran between solid rows of people. In New York, 100,000 marched in a mourning parade while half a million looked on. The land had gone wild! Newspapers seemed stunned, groping for words to describe what was happening.

News of the extravagance with which the funeral train was being received whipped the next cities into a frenzy. Now competition set in as the decorations had to be larger, the crowds bigger, and the speakers more eloquent in their adulation of the fallen President. By the time the cortege reached Cleveland, Ohio, all restraint vanished, as civic rivalry grew.

Indiana shamed Ohio, just as Ohio had shamed New York, and New York had shamed Pennsylvania. Then it was Illinois' turn, and the outpourings reached a crescendo. Such was the madness of the moment that mourners swarmed over the hearse and had to be bayoneted back by the honor guard.

Finally the President was laid to rest, but the nation was not ready to leave the matter there, especially after James Redpath, superintendent of the freedmen's schools in Charleston, South Carolina, held his ceremony. On May 1, 1865, he led over 10,000 former slaves to a cemetery that had been laid out to hold the remains of Union soldiers who had died in a Confederate prison camp. With their arms full of blossoms and singing John Brown's body, they laid their flowers at the graves in honor of "Marsa Linco'n."

This story was traveling on the telegraph lines within hours, and not to be outdone, cities all over the North began to hold similar observances. This rivalry continued until General John A. Logan, head of the Grand Army of the Republic, declared that May 30 would be observed every year as Memorial Day, honoring not only the memory of President Lincoln but of all the Civil War dead.

Thus it was that on the day they buried Abraham Lincoln's travel-worn body in Illinois amid all that funeral hysteria, the first Memorial Day observance was being held in–of all places—Charleston, South Carolina, by 10,000 African Americans.

THE VICE PRESIDENT WHO NEVER MADE IT HOME

William Rufus King was born to be a politician. This public servant represented the people of North Carolina in the United States House of Representatives and later those from Alabama in the United States Senate. He reached the zenith of his political career when he was elected to the office of Vice President of the United States. Strangely enough, however, this man who was just one heart beat from the Presidency never set foot in Washington D.C. after he and Franklin Pierce won the election of 1852—not even when it came time for him to take the oath of office.

William Rufus King

King was born in 1786, in North Carolina. From his early years, he seemed destined for greatness. After graduating from private schools in Sampson County, he continued his brilliant academic career at the University of North Carolina and then studied law. He was admitted to the bar and almost immediately entered into public service.

From 1807 to 1809 King held a seat in the State House of Commons. In 1810, he was elected to Congress and served in that body until 1816, when he resigned to enter the diplomatic corps. After representing the United States at Naples and St. Petersburg, Russia, King returned to the United States and established a plantation in Cahaba, Alabama.

Although King enjoyed the life of a southern planter, he had politics in his blood. When Alabama became a state in 1819, he was elected to the United States Senate. He was reelected in 1822, 1828, 1834, and 1840.

In 1844, he gave up his seat in the Senate to reenter the diplomatic corps, this time as Minister to France, a position he held until 1846.

When William Rufus King returned to Alabama, the people sent him back to Washington to resume his work as their senator, and he remained at his post until that pivotal election of 1852.

Everybody assumed that either Lewis Cass or James Buchanan would win the Democratic nomination and the election, but they had overlooked the dark horse candidacy of Franklin Pierce and his running mate, William Rufus King.

Pierce and King amassed 254 electoral votes and prepared for Inauguration Day. Just at the height of putting together a new administration, however, fate dealt a blow to the incoming Vice President. He fell deathly ill and resigned his seat in the United States Senate to seek a recovery of his health in Cuba.

Thus it was that the Vice President Elect of the United States went to Havana and missed his inauguration in Washington. For you see, William Rufus King never got well. He was so sick that Congress had to enact special legislation for him to take the oath of office in Cuba, which was accomplished on March 24, 1853, twenty days after the official Inauguration Day in Washington D.C.

A week later King was well enough to return to Alabama, but that was as close as he got to Washington. They took him to "King's Bend," his Alabama plantation, where on April 18, 1853, he passed away. In a tragic twist in time, William simply ran out of time. He had been Vice President of the United States for 25 days but he never made it to the nation's capital to perform a single official duty.

HOW FREE LOVE EXTRACTED ITS POUND OF FLESH

Charles Guiteau

    America at the mid-point of the 19th century was a haven for reformers. Some were legitimately attempting to eliminate inequality and foster mutual benefit societies. Others, however, like the Oneida Community, went off the deep end and demanded that members not only share their property but their women as well. This practice of "complex marriages," which was nothing more than a philosophy of "free love," may have worked for some, but it pushed young Charles over the edge and wound up sending a nation into mourning.
    The Oneida Community was founded by John Humphrey Noyes. Although he dabbled in theology, this was not his foremost interest. He was much more taken with the

idea of playing sexual musical chairs with his followers. This is what excited Charles about Noyes' community lifestyle.

There can be no doubt that the young man was attracted by the community's doctrine of free love. Although he was small and unattractive, he convinced himself that he would be welcomed with open arms by the Oneida women. Here was a place where he would finally be appreciated.

Besides that, he had $900 dollars in his pocket, which he turned over to the community, hoping that this would further ingratiate him among the ranks of the fairer sex. How wrong he was!

Although everybody in the community was encouraged to share sexual favors with any member of the opposite sex, nobody jumped at the chance for a night with Charles. The women made fun of him and nicknamed him Charles "Git Out." This of course was not acceptable and sent Charles into a psychological tailspin from which he never recovered. Friction soon developed between him and most everyone else in the community. He even scrawled a line of chalk across the dormitory floor and insisted that his roommate not cross it.

Charles then demanded that Noyes return his $900, which the commune leader refused to do. In retaliation, Charles issued a press release to the effect that Noyes had "personally deflowered every virgin in the Oneida Community," leaving none for a young man such as himself. This got him a quick exit from the Oneida Community.

Charles then went into a period of deep depression after his rejection at Oneida and began to develop all sorts of delusional fantasies, not the least of which was his idea that the government required his services as a diplomat in Vienna. When nobody responded to his offer to serve, Charles moved to Washington, and spent a great deal of time trying to convince the President that he was exactly the sort of man this nation needed to represent itself abroad. Once more he felt rejection, and this he could not handle.

On July 2, 1881, Charles was able to reach the President in the train station next to Capitol Hill and put a bullet into his body, which took the life of the chief executive three months later.

Thus did America lose a second President to an assassin, but the story was cleaned up for the classrooms. It was much more proper to teach that Charles Giteau killed James A. Garfield because he was a disgruntled civil servant than to admit that his rejection in the free love community of Oneida was what sent him spinning into the fickle arms of fate and onto the pages of history.

POLITICAL TREACHERY IN BALTIMORE

The name of Hannibal Hamlin is not exactly a household word, but perhaps it should be. The man spent most of his adult life in the service of his country, and when the Civil War began to tear the nation apart, Hamlin was right there to help save it. For four tumultuous years he stood loyally beside President's Lincoln's side as his Vice President. Then came the Republican convention of 1864. Hamlin was sure he would be Lincoln's running mate again, but he had no way of knowing that one of his most trusted friends was about to send him into obscurity.

Hannibal Hamlin performed a yeoman's service as Abraham Lincoln's second in command. He talked William Seward and Gideon Welles into joining the cabinet. He pushed Lincoln to issue the Emancipation Proclamation, and he urged the President to enlist Blacks in the Union Army. No doubt about it, Hamlin went above and beyond the call of duty as Vice President. Then came that disaster in Baltimore.

In the election of 1864, General George McClellan carried the Democratic banner, and President Lincoln easily won nomination for a second term, but when it came time for the Republicans to choose a running mate, Hamlin was thrown to the wolves. The convention chose a Democrat, Andrew Johnson, to replace him as Lincoln's Vice President.

If Hamlin was surprised when he was denied a second term, he was dumbfounded when he found out precisely how he had been dumped. It had all been a tightly woven intrigue perpetrated by someone he trusted. His friend, who took

Hannibal Hamlin

no public part in the debates or campaigning, had nevertheless conducted a ferocious whispering war.

The turncoat pointed out that since Hamlin was from Maine, his political capital was near zero, since the Republicans already had that section of the country locked up without him. The betrayer also impugned Hamlin's usefulness by secretly reminding delegates that the Vice President's radical record on civil rights had made him a political liability. The Machiavellian detractor claimed the party needed a former slave owning, Southern Democrat who had a soft spot in his heart for Rebels, and that is exacting what it got.

Now just who was this purveyor of calumny in 1864? Who was it that slyly and secretly poisoned the well for Hannibal Hamlin? It was none other than Abraham Lincoln!

Thus it was, you see, that Andrew Johnson from Tennessee replaced Hannibal Hamlin as Abraham Lincoln's Vice President. In a stunning twist in time, Old Honest Abe forgot about loyalty and friendship for a moment and opted for political expediency instead. Sometimes war will do strange things to people

THE PRESIDENT WHO ROCKED THE CRADLE

The President's Wedding

When Oscar Folsom, a Buffalo, New York attorney, chose young Grover Cleveland as his law partner in 1863, most folks thought that he had made a good choice. The younger barrister was hard working, smart, and loyal to a fault. In fact, Cleveland was so loyal that after Oscar's death in a buggy accident in 1875, he embraced his partner's family as his own. He promised the Widow Folsom that he would take real good care of her and her eleven year-old daughter, Frances. In time the whole world found out that the future President was every bit as good as his word.

Grover Cleveland, who became the administrator of Folsom's estate and unofficial guardian of his daughter, took his responsibilities seriously. He saw to his adopted family's every need and grew ever closer to Folsom's widow, Emma, and her daughter, who called their family provider, "Uncle Cleve."

Over the years Cleveland began to climb the political ladder. In 1881, he was elected Mayor of Buffalo and later Governor of New York, but he never allowed his official duties to diminish his devotion to Emma and Frances. He paid for the daughter's education at private schools, academies, and eventually to Wells College, and he saw to it that Emma wanted for nothing.

Then in 1884, the unthinkable happened. A Democrat was elected President of the United States. For the first time since 1856, the people turned their backs on the Republicans, and they did so by voting for Grover Cleveland.

In March 1885, Cleveland moved into the White House, but he soon found out he required a helpmate. He could handle the duties of the Presidency, but he needed a First Lady. Naturally his mind went back to Buffalo.

He had only been President for five months when he sent for Emma and Frances. The official word was that he was simply inviting old friends to visit the White House, but the press corps couldn't be fooled. They suspected that the President would be making a proposal for marriage, and they were right. When they reported the gossip, the country went positively giddy. Emma would make a charming First Lady, and her beautiful longhaired daughter--what a glamorous addition to the White House she would make.

Grover Cleveland did offer that proposal for marriage, and when he sent Emma and Frances on a tour of Europe, the reporters followed them, eagerly trying to scoop each other as to the wedding date. Little did they know what the White House had in store for them.

When Emma and Frances returned, Cleveland made

the official announcement. There was going to be a marriage in the White House. The nation was finally going to get a First Lady, but it wasn't going to be the Widow Folsom. It was going to be her daughter!

On June 2, 1886, forty-nine year-old Grover Cleveland married twenty-one year-old Frances Folsom in a White House ceremony and in doing so, the groom set a number of precedents. He was the first President to be married in the White House. He was the first President who could honestly say he met his future bride while she was still wearing diapers, and he was the first President to actually provide his future wife with a baby stroller in which she could ride.

In a surprising twist in time Grover Cleveland may not have robbed the cradle, but he sure did rock it.

DRAMA FOLLOWS LINCOLN TO WASHINGTON

In May 1860, the eyes of the nation were on Chicago where the Republicans were holding their second quadrennial convention. There were five major contenders for the Party's presidential nomination that year, and the front runner was William H. Seward. As things turned out, Senator Seward was denied the honor and had to yield to the shrewd maneuvering of the floor managers for Abraham Lincoln.

Illinois' favorite son won on the third ballot, and the hall went wild. Meanwhile just a few blocks down the street the curtain went up on an eerie harbinger of the future, as if it were heralding a tragedy that would bring the Republicans to their knees five years later.

Following the protocol of the times, none of the contenders were in Chicago for the convention. Instead, each sent his own delegation of supporters to wage political war in the aisles for votes, and fight they did!

Seward expected to win on the first ballot; all the Senator's handlers had to do was convince 233 delegates to vote for him, and the nomination was his. Unfortunately for Seward, he fell 60 votes short. On that first tally Lincoln grabbed 102, Simon Cameron got 50, Salmon Chase garnered 49, and Edward Bates snatched 48. The remainder went to several favorite sons.

That first vote made it obvious that the contest had boiled down to a tug-o-war between Seward and Lincoln, so their supporters went scrambling for votes. On the next night during the second ballot, Seward increased his number to 184, but Lincoln was breathing down his neck with 181. Now the nomination was a tossup, and the convention prepared for the next night's finale.

When the third ballot ended with Lincoln holding the votes of 231 ½ delegates, just 1 ½ short of the required 233, a hush fell over the hall. Suspense reigned supreme until the Ohio delegation took four votes from Chase, its favorite son, and gave them to Lincoln. With that, pandemonium broke loose. The cracker-barrel philosopher had beaten the odds; he would become the 16th President of the United States.

Amidst all of the political revelry, none of the delegates took time to notice what was going on down the street at McVicker's Theatre that night, and there was really no reason for them to do so. The performance was nothing out of the ordinary—except that it would one day be burned into the hearts and minds of Americans forever. For you see, the play that opened on the night that Abraham Lincoln first won the Republican presidential nomination was none other than *"Our American Cousin."* In a spine tingling twist in time, it would one day play again, this time at Ford's theatre, and Lincoln would be watching it during his last night on earth.

Drama Follows Lincoln to Washington

ONE MAN'S COSTLY EPITAPH

William H. Seward

In Auburn, New York's Fort Hill Cemetery lie the remains of a man who came within a hair of occupying the White House. He was favored to win the nomination of his party for President of the United States and might have done so if only his epitaph had not been written years before. Today one can read on his tombstone the words, "He was Faithful." Contrary to the dictates of common sense, it was precisely this sentiment that cost the man the Presidency in 1860.

It all began in March 1846, with a terrifying massacre in Auburn, New York. William Freeman, a 23 year-old black man, entered the home of John Van Nest, a wealthy resident of the town, and stabbed the farmer, his pregnant wife, their small child, and Mrs. Van Nest's mother. The murderer was quickly caught and just as quickly revealed that he was totally bereft of any reasoning ability. If ever an insanity defense could be mounted, Freeman's case warranted it. The only trouble was that no one would defend the accused. That's when the Faithful One stepped forth.

Everyone advised the lawyer against taking the case. Family and friends alike roundly criticized him for his decision. Still he pressed forward with his defense.

There was never any doubt that the jury would render a guilty verdict. The crime was just too gruesome, and the accused was Black. In his summation, the defense attorney intoned, "In due time, gentleman of the jury...my remains will rest here in your midst....perhaps when the passion...shall have passed away, some wandering stranger...may erect over them a humble stone and thereon [engrave] this epitaph, 'He was Faithful.'"

The Freeman case stirred the emotions of the country, and brought the lawyer considerable support among the anti-slavery people. However, there were others who thought he had gone too far. Making speeches against slavery was one thing, but to defend the black murderer of one's friend was quite another. These moderates never forgot.

Over the next fourteen years, the lawyer enjoyed a remarkable rise in political fortunes. He was elected Governor of New York, and in 1849 the state sent him to the United States Senate. Then in 1860, just as his political star had reached its zenith, he was put forth as a candidate for the Republican Party's presidential nomination.

Everyone expected him to win on the first ballot, and he would have if only all of the delegates could have forgotten the Freeman case. As it was, 60 of them sent their votes in another direction, and by the third ballot it was all over. The Party chose a man who was more moderate regarding slavery and who had never taken up the cause of the civil rights of Blacks. Abraham Lincoln fit the bill.

The New York politician was not forgotten, however. He went on to make his mark on the pages of American history, for you see, the man who dictated his own epitaph in front of that Freeman jury in 1846—the man who lost his chance at the Presidency because of that epitaph--was William H. Seward, Lincoln's Secretary of State. In a prophetic twist in time, he predicted what his tombstone would say. One has to wonder if he had any inkling of its political ramifications.

TAFT'S LEGACY WENT BEYOND THE BATHROOM

William H. Taft

History has not been kind to William Howard Taft, 27th President of the United States. Today he is best remembered for that embarrassing episode in which he managed to wedge his 350-pound frame in the White House bathtub and had to wait for the fire department to rescue him. A more serious look at Taft, however, reveals that he left much more of a legacy for Americans than his dilemma in the lavatory. His love affair with professional baseball gave the nation two traditions that should have overshadowed his weight problem.

President Taft followed major league baseball with a passion, and his favorite team was not surprisingly the Washington Senators. That is why he was at Griffith Stadium on April 14, 1910. Taft's team was playing the Philadelphia Athletics, so the President slipped away from his desk to attend the game. As things turned out, he changed baseball forever.

The stands were filled that day and the lively crowd yelled and screamed when the rival managers were introduced. Then as the game was about to begin, umpire Billy Evans walked over to the President's box and handed Taft the baseball with the request that he throw it over home plate. With great relish, the President threw the ball to the catcher, and the spectators roared their approval, never knowing that they had just witnessed the launching of a national tradition. Since that time, every United States President except Jimmy Carter has started a baseball season during his term of office by throwing out the first ball at the first game. This, however, was just the beginning. Before Taft left the ballpark that day he established yet another baseball tradition.

As the face-off between the Senators and the Athletics wore on, the rotund, six-foot-two Chief Executive grew increasingly uneasy in his tiny wooden chair. With each inning he became more and more restless until finally he could bear it no longer. Seeking some relief from his throbbing legs, he stood up to stretch them, and as he gazed around, he saw the crowd doing likewise. Thinking that he was preparing to leave, the spectators rose to their feet to show their respect. When Taft returned to his seat to watch the conclusion of the game, the people did the same.

The next day, as the newspapers dutifully recorded both the "opening pitch" by the President and his prolonged stretch, which had occurred in the seventh inning, baseball promoters immediately seized their golden opportunity. If it was good for the President and the crowd at Griffith Stadium, it was good for the country and good for the game, so in a popular twist in time, baseball fans still take a seventh inning stretch, and the President still throws out the first pitch. It is too bad William Howard Taft doesn't get credit for setting these precedents. Perhaps then folks would forget about his private privy experience.

TEDDY ROOSEVELT'S COFFEE HOUSE PROVERB

In 1907 ★★ Theodore Roosevelt said "*Good to the Last Drop!*"

Theodore Roosevelt

    Theodore Roosevelt is remembered as much for his one-liners as he is for his achievements as the nation's 26th President. No American can forget his maxim, "Speak softly and carry a big stick," or his admonition, "Don't hit a man if you can possibly avoid it, but if you do hit him, put him to sleep." Roosevelt's well-known aphorisms have become part of his legacy. However, one of his most popular sayings is repeated almost every day without folks knowing that it was Teddy who coined the phrase in 1903.

    In that year, Roosevelt went on a tour of the country, which took him to Nashville, Tennessee. As was the custom with almost every person of renown who visited the town, Teddy lodged in the same ornate, antebellum hotel that had housed at least seven presidents and such celebrities as Thomas Edison, Buffalo Bill, and Tom Thumb.

The hotel had been the pride of Nashville since before the Civil War and served as a social mecca for over 100 years. It had been built in 1856 by Colonel John Overton Jr. for his wife, and at first people thought it to be much too opulent for a city of only 16,000 residents. Time, however, proved its detractors wrong, especially when its guest list included Rutherford B. Hayes, Grover Cleveland, and William McKinley.

Nashville's famous hotel had much to commend it to high society. In addition to lavishly furnished rooms, it offered its pampered guests the ultimate in service, but its real claim to fame was its coffee. Especially prepared by the hotel's kitchen staff, the very smell of the morning brew brought Nashville's fancy visitors alive and a sip or two was described as pure elixir.

On the first morning of his first visit to the hotel, Roosevelt, who never was sluggish about getting up in the morning, received an unexpected lift from his first cup of house coffee. The President savored those dregs and then asked for more. When he saw the bottom of his last cup, he turned to his attendant and in characteristic fashion pontificated that the brew was "good to the last drop," and that's how the theme for Maxwell House coffee came into being.

For you see, the hotel in which the President was staying was the Maxwell House, named for its owner's wife, Harriet Maxwell. In a delicious twist in time, President Theodore Roosevelt gave the establishment's coffee such a boost with his "good to the last drop" testimonial, that it soon found a national market. Before long everyone was singing the praises of Maxwell House coffee and proclaiming that it was "good to the last drop," and thus it remains to this very day, thanks to Teddy Roosevelt and his way with words.

TEDDY ROOSEVELT'S
DOUBLE WHAMMY

Martha Bulloch Roosevelt

President Theodore Roosevelt adored his mother, Martha Mittie Bulloch Roosevelt. As a child, he sat at her knee and drank in the stories of her childhood in the Old South with its mint juleps, hanging moss, and its palatial plantations. It comes as no surprise then that he took great care to watch out for her after his father's death.

On the afternoon of February 14, 1884, Mittie passed away, and Theodore was rocked to the core. Fate, however, was not through with him yet. Before the sun set that day the future President would receive a second shock from which he would never recover.

Shortly after his graduation from Harvard University in 1880, Roosevelt married the love of his life, Alice Hathaway Lee. They set up housekeeping in his home on 57th Street in New York City and soon took in his mother to live with them. It was an idyllic existence for the two lovers, who were not at all bothered by the presence of Mittie.

In 1881, the people elected Theodore to represent them in the State Assembly, so he divided his time between New York City and Albany. Roosevelt acquitted himself admirably, both in the legislature and at home. The three adults formed one happy family, and when Alice announced that she was pregnant, everyone was delirious.

Theodore was serving his third term in the Assembly when the baby arrived on February 12, 1884. When Alice Lee delivered her daughter without complications, Roosevelt turned his attention to his mother. She had come down with typhoid and became dangerously ill. For two days and two nights, the young father alternated between his wife's bedroom and his mother's.

Two days after his wife brought his daughter into this world, Roosevelt's mother left it. She succumbed to the fever in that house on 57th Street. Theodore was of course grief-stricken, but as he sat beside the still body of his mother, the doctor intruded to give him the news that completely devastated him. Not only had he lost his mother; his wife had just died as well.

You see, Alice Lee had been afflicted with Bright's disease, which had been masked by her pregnancy. Chronic kidney infection set in unexpectedly, and it killed her. In an unbelievable twist in time Theodore Roosevelt lost his wife and his mother on the same day in the same house.

The inconsolable Roosevelt turned his back on the world that he knew for two years, and when he remarried in 1886, he would not allow anyone to utter the name of his beloved Alice. Apparently the mind--even Teddy Roosevelt's--is limited in the amount of pain it can handle

HOW A DREAM ALMOST COST A PRESIDENT HIS LIFE

Roosevelt as NY Police Commissioner

When John F. Schrank went to bed on the night of September 14, 1901, he was tossing and turning—in fact, America was tossing and turning—for President William McKinley, after having been shot by an assassin several days earlier, had died. Schrank finally went to sleep that night, but about 1:30 in the morning he woke up from a dream in which the fallen President had appeared to him. That dream changed Schrank's life and came within an inch of changing the course of American history.

At the time John Schrank was twenty-six years old, short, and something of a recluse. He had a room above the saloon in which he had been employed until the police commissioner of New York City led a crusade against the operation of taverns on Sunday. As a result Schrank lost his job and was never able to fully recover. He always blamed the police commissioner for his financial troubles.

Now as he remembered his dream, Schrank had found himself in a funeral parlor full of flowers. Before him lay an open casket and in it lay President William McKinley. In his dream, as Schrank stood paying his respects to the dead president, McKinley suddenly sat up and pointed to a dark corner of the room. John looked in the direction in which the corpse was pointing and saw a figure dressed in a monk's raiment. Beneath the cowl Schrank was able to make out the detested visage of the police commissioner who had robbed him of his livelihood.

Suddenly McKinley spoke, "There is my murderer," and Schrank woke up in a cold sweat. He finally got back to sleep, but he never forgot his nocturnal apparition.

For the next decade, Schrank flitted from job to job without making anything of himself. Then on September 14, 1912, the 11th anniversary of McKinley's assassination, Schrank was up late at night when he thought he felt a tap on his shoulder. He later said he heard a voice and when he turned he saw the image of William McKinley and heard the fallen President instruct him to avenge his death. That's when Schrank decided to shoot Theodore Roosevelt.

For you see, it was the former President who had once been New York City's police commissioner and whom Schrank held responsible for closing up the saloons on Sunday and costing him his livelihood.

In a fateful twist in time, Schrank found Roosevelt in Milwaukee, Wisconsin and put a bullet in his chest. The former President survived, but Schrank never knew it. He spent the rest of his life in a mental institution thinking he had killed Roosevelt, and how did he know? Why else would William McKinley continue to visit him in his hospital dreams with paeans of praise for his solitary, selfless act of bravery?

INEBRIATION AT LINCOLN'S INAUGURATION

Andrew Johnson

On March 4, 1865, Abraham Lincoln, not knowing that he had just 43 days to live, could not have been happier. His face fairly beamed from the victory he had wretched from George McClellan the previous November. Now crowds had gathered at the capitol for his second inaugural address. Before he could speak, however, the ceremony took a ludicrous turn due to the antics of one of the officials who had managed to get himself quite drunk!

Shortly before Noon the nation's "notables"— generals, governors, Supreme Court justices, cabinet members, and finally President Lincoln arrived. They were all seated quite properly according to rank, and the ceremony began.

Everything proceeded smoothly until Hannibal Hamlin concluded his remarks. At that point a man, who was barely able to maintain his balance, stumbled to the podium. His "state of manifest intoxication" was evident for all to see. While Lincoln sat stoically and looking straight ahead, everyone else held their breath.

When the tipsy fellow began to speak, his words tumbled incoherently from his mouth. He mumbled something about his log cabin beginnings not being a hindrance to his rise in politics and that in spite of his plebeian background, he had every right to be among those gathered that day. The assembled guests shot quick glances at the President, who remained impervious to the spectacle.

After ten long, rambling minutes, the speaker turned to give the dignitaries a lecture. As he pivoted to face the Supreme Court justices, he admonished them to never forget that they derived their power from the people. Then he tried to address each member of the cabinet by name,--Mr. Seward,

Mr. Stanton, and down the ranks until he reached Gideon Welles. There his befuddled mind hit a brick wall. He couldn't remember the man's name. Seemingly nonplussed, he loudly inquired as to the name of the Secretary of the Navy.

When the drunk continued his tirade in spite of a whispered warning from Hamlin that he was disrupting the ceremony, the crowd shifted uncomfortably. All heads turned toward Lincoln who, with eyes shut so as to hide his own discomfort, patiently waited for the harangue to end. Mercifully, after 20 minutes the tippler closed his meandering speech, but he didn't sit down.

You see, the drunk who roamed across the platform that day was none other than Andrew Johnson, the newly elected Vice President of the United States. Apparently the honor which was being bestowed upon him had driven him to fortify himself to excess. In an intoxicating twist in time, the Tennessee politician who would have the Presidency thrust upon him in less than two months, had to turn to the bottle for courage just to take the oath of office.

Is it any wonder then that the country trembled a few weeks later when John Wilkes Booth placed such a man in the White House?

Civil War Oddities
With A Twist

A REBEL IN THE WHITE HOUSE

Emilie Todd Helm's White House Bedroom

On September 21, 1863, Confederate General Benjamin Hardin Helm was killed in the Battle of Chickamauga. Word of his death was immediately carried to his wife, Emilie, who was residing temporarily in Alabama. The news so devastated Mrs. Helm that she decided to attempt to leave the South to seek succor in the home of her sister in Washington, D.C. It took some doing for Emilie to get through the lines, but she finally made it to the Capital. When she did, however, her presence caused such a furor that she almost wished she had stayed in Alabama.

Emilie had left her home in Lexington, Kentucky, when the firing on Fort Sumter thrust the nation into the beginning of its four-year blood bath. Her husband, Benjamin Helm, had turned down a commission in the Union Army and headed south to fight for the Confederacy. He took Emilie with him and left her with friends in Alabama while he marched off to war. Now more than two years later she found herself a widow in the Yankee Capital.

When Emilie arrived at her sister's house, she was received with warm and open arms. There was no talk between the women about their having married men who stood firmly on opposite sides in the War Between the States. Then word leaked out that a Confederate general's widow was living in Washington, D.C. A political uproar went up all over town, so Emilie's sister appealed to President Abraham Lincoln.

Now it just so happened that a week earlier Lincoln had issued his Proclamation of Amnesty and Reconstruction, which restored United States citizenship to any Southerner, except the highest Confederate officials, who would disavow his or her allegiance to the Rebel Government. In an effort to quell the unrest over Emilie's presence in Washington, Lincoln issued a pardon to her under the provisions of his proclamation. That might have settled the issue, had it not been for Major General Daniel Sickles.

The General, who had lost a leg in the Battle of Gettysburg just a few months before, was vociferous in his opposition to Lincoln's pardon for Emilie. He hobbled over to the White House from the Willard Hotel to inform the President that the Capital should not be a haven for refugee rebels. The President replied, "General Sickles, my wife and I are in the habit of choosing our own guests. We do not need from our friends either advice or assistance in the matter."

The General was shocked, for you see, the sister who had opened up her home to Emilie was none other than Mary Todd Lincoln. In an unexpected twist in time, when Emilie left Alabama, she headed straight for the White House and was taken in by the Lincolns.

Some people continued to gossip about the presence of a "rebel spy" in the White House, but Lincoln held firm. Finally, Emilie decided to leave Washington and return to Lexington. She had gained a new respect for the President who could on the one hand take comfort in the killing of one more Confederate General and still give unqualified refuge to his widow.

GENERAL GRANT READ THE SIGNS

In the days before the use of sophisticated Special Forces and the appearance of modern intelligence-gathering apparatus, the United States military often had to rely solely upon the ingenuity of its officers. Generals—especially Civil War Generals—had to use tiny bits of information to out think their opponents and win battles, like Ulysses S. Grant did as he prepared to assault Fort Donelson in 1862.

The capture of Fort Donelson on the Cumberland River and Fort Henry on the Tennessee River was key to Grant's plan to move south and ultimately take control of the Mississippi River, thus separating Texas, Arkansas, and Louisiana from the rest of the Confederacy.

Grant first dealt with Fort Henry. After a short siege, on February 6, 1862, he took the garrison, but not before most of the enemy troops escaped east to reinforce his next objective. Grant immediately turned his troops toward Fort Donelson and put them on a forced march through the swamps that separated the two Confederate strongholds. It took Grant's army, marching in rain and bitter cold, nine days to reach the fortress on the Cumberland River, which by then had been reinforced by those rebel soldiers who had escaped from Ft. Henry. There on February 15, 1862, Grant was faced with a dilemma.

He suspected that Fort Donelson had been reinforced, but he wasn't sure just how much fight Johnny Reb had left in him. Should he take a chance and order his exhausted men to attack the fort on the assumption that the enemy had lost much of his fighting spirit, or should he give his men a rest, which would also give the rebels time to recover from their defeat at Fort Henry?

As Grant pondered the situation and weighed the alternatives, an orderly came to his tent with the news that a rebel deserter had been captured while attempting to sneak out of Fort Donelson. Perhaps this was Grant's chance to gather inside information. He called for the deserter. In a moment a scared, scrawny soldier stood before the General.

Surprisingly the runaway was reluctant to supply Grant with any real information on conditions inside the fort. Apparently he had recovered some sense of his obligation as a soldier. Frustrated, Grant grabbed the soldier's knapsack and examined its contents. The General thought for a moment and then straightway ordered an attack on Fort Donelson. He now knew that the enemy was ready to give up.

Before the next day was over, Fort Donelson had surrendered. Grant had figured correctly; there had been no more fight in the rebel defenders, but how did he know? For Grant it had been simple.

You see, the deserter's haversack had contained six days rations. When the General learned from the rebel runaway that they had been served out the day before and that every soldier had received the same six-day's supply, Grant knew that the rebels were through. In a calculating twist in time, the General told his staff, "Gentlemen, troops do not have six day's rations served out to them in a fort if they mean to stay there. These men meant to retreat—not fight."

Thus did Ulysses S. Grant divine the intent of the enemy—not with spies, not with radar, nor any other device of modern warfare, but with a little intuition and common sense—not a bad combination for success.

General Ulysses S. Grant

GETTYSBURG AND THE CANDY MAN

Milton Hershey

The roar of the cannon came from the southwest where two huge armies swayed back and forth in a death grip. The fate of the nation was being decided at Gettysburg, and a barefoot boy was trudging behind a wagon along a dusty Pennsylvania road in an attempt to flee the horror of war. The date was July 2, 1863.

The young lad turned his eyes toward an ancient stone mansion, the home of his father and grandfather. Then he passed the old house his great-grandfather had built on land that had been granted him by William Penn. The boy was just seven years old, and the violent Civil War struggle was driving him from his childhood surroundings--but only temporarily.

The lad went on, kicked up dust and muttered, "I betchya when I get to be worth a million, billion, trillion dollars, I'll be back."

Well, the war ended, and the boy went out into the world. He was molded by his wartime experience and determined to make good. At first he found work as a printer's helper, and then he got a job in a candy store. Once he had learned the art of caramel making, he started his own factory, and in time he made so much money that he claimed he didn't want any more, so he decided to return to the farm from which he had walked while the battle of Gettysburg was raging. He went back to buy the land that had once belonged to his father, grandfather, and great-grandfather.

When this was accomplished, the boy, now grown into a nationally known business tycoon, discovered that the biggest opportunity of all existed right there on his ancestral farm. He was right in the middle of dairy country, so he came out of retirement, started a little chocolate factory, and built a town around the home of his forefathers.

That is how Hershey, Pennsylvania, got started, and that is how America got a brand new candy bar, for you see, that little fellow who fled the armies of Robert E. Lee and George Meade was none other than Milton Hershey. In a delicious twist in time, the lad fulfilled his lifetime wish to return home and in the process became a multi-millionaire, a philanthropist, and America's Chocolate King.

HOW JACKSON LOST A BATTLE BUT MADE A NAME FOR HIMSELF

William L. Jackson

The Civil War battle of Bulltown was fought in Braxton County, West Virginia, at a strategic crossing of the Little Kanawha River. Union forces had built a semi-permanent garrison on a hill overlooking the road that crossed the stream, and Colonel William L. Jackson of the 19th Virginia Cavalry decided to destroy the hastily built mud fort. The Rebels gave it a good try, but at the end of the day, the Yankees still had their fort, and the Confederate Colonel had a new name.

On the evening of October 12, 1863, Colonel Jackson reached the Little Kanawah at Falls Mills. He planned to divide his command in two detachments and to attack the fortification at daybreak. He assigned Major J. M. Kessler to approach from the northeast, while the Colonel would come up from the southwest. Both men were to attack at the same time, but the plan for some reason miscarried.

When Kessler arrived first with his men, he did not wait for Jackson. At 4:30 in the morning he attacked and was repulsed. When Jackson did arrive in position and saw that things were not going exactly as planned, he decided to play his trump card and bluff. Sending a message to the top of the hill under a flag of truce, he demanded that the commander of the fortification surrender. The answer Jackson received was not exactly what he had expected. The Union commander invited Jackson to "Come and get us."

Well, all day long he tried, but that earlier charge by Kessler had taken some of the fight out of the boys. They all realized that taking the Bulltown fort was not going to be a pushover. Charge after charge was made up the hill, but the Union troops remained well ensconced behind those thick, mud walls that surrounded the blockhouse. In the minds of Jackson's men, the enemy was unassailable.

Frustrated in his attempts to take the hill or to make the Yankees realize the hopelessness of their situation, Jackson ordered a resumption of firing that continued to twilight. Finally recognizing that hardheaded Billy Yank was not going to give up and that he had expended most of his ammunition, the Colonel accepted reality and called off the assault. His dreams of glory had been squashed by the mud walls of the Bulltown fort.

Jackson's disgusted troops were able to appreciate the irony of the situation. They promptly dubbed their frustrated commander, "Mudwall" just to make certain that no one confused him with his recently deceased relative.

His failure to take the Bulltown garrison apparently had no affect on his reputation in the War Department. Colonel Jackson was soon promoted to Brigadier General, and after the war, he held several prestigious positions in government, but he was never able to shed the sobriquet that had been bestowed upon him at Bulltown, and he would always stand in the shadow of his more famous kinsman.

For you see, "Mudwall" Jackson was a first cousin to General "Stonewall" Jackson. In a trying twist in time, the former attempted to match the heroics of the latter but found it impossible to live up to his reputation. In the end he had to settle for a nickname that it itself told the whole story.

A WOMAN SUCCEEDS WHILE THE MEN DAWDLE

Major Robert Anderson

In April of 1861, nerves were frayed as the country cast its eyes toward South Carolina. The newly formed Confederate army had occupied Federal forts all over the South and threatened Fort Moultrie in Charleston. For that reason, Major Robert Anderson moved his men inside the protective walls of Fort Sumter, in the middle of Charleston Harbor. For the moment the garrison was safely in the hands of the Union, but there was a problem. Provisions were perilously low, and there appeared no way to reinforce the fort without starting the war that President Lincoln was desperately trying to avoid. Then up stepped a woman who gave the nation's men a lesson in dogged determination and ingenuity.

No one was more worried about the situation than Major Anderson's invalid wife, who was living in New York at the time. She knew that her husband faced a tenacious, ferocious foe, but she was more afraid of possible traitors from within. That is why she went looking for Peter Hart, who had served under her husband in the Mexican War. She resolved to find the trusted former sergeant and place him by Major Anderson's side as his bodyguard within the walls of Fort Sumter.

It took Mrs. Anderson a day and a half to find Hart, but as soon as she shared her concern with him, they boarded a train for an unpleasant ride to Charleston. The cars were filled with rebels who were hastening to join the attack on Fort Sumter. She could neither eat, drink, nor sleep amidst the constant chatter of threats against her husband.

When the pair arrived in Charleston, they ran into a major roadblock. Mrs. Anderson had no problem obtaining permission from Governor Francis Pickens to visit Fort Sumter, but she was refused a permit for Sergeant Hart. Pickens reminded her that he had declared that he would not allow the garrison to be reinforced—not even by a solitary ex-soldier.

At this point, Mrs. Anderson turned on the Governor in a fit of rage. She demanded to know how South Carolinians could maintain their highly touted honor as citizens of a sovereign power when they feared that the addition of one man would threaten their position, especially when thousands of armed men stood by on shore ready and willing to strike at Fort Sumter.

It took the Governor only a moment to recognize the absurdity of his refusal, so he provided a pass for Hart as well. With that, the sergeant and Mrs. Anderson were rowed out to the fort under a flag of truce. Her husband met them, and Mrs. Anderson reciprocated the Major's greetings with a simple remark, "I have brought you Peter Hart. The children are well; I now return."

As Anderson and Hart made their way inside the fort, Mrs. Anderson got back in the skiff and returned to Charleston. That same evening she departed for Washington D.C. where she provided a stunned War Department with the details of her mission.

For you see, this brave woman had done what the United States Government was unable to do. In an ironic twist in time, she had not sent, but had taken, reinforcement to Fort Sumter without a shot being fired.

YOU CAN'T TAKE THE SOUTH OUT OF THE BOY

Teddy Roosevelt

On Tuesday, April 25th, 1865, it was New York City's turn to pay its respects to the nation's martyred President Abraham Lincoln. His remains were being carried on a 1,700-mile journey to his hometown of Springfield, Illinois, for burial. Like Washington, D.C., Baltimore, Harrisburg, and Philadelphia before it, thousands turned out for New York's gigantic funeral procession. Eleven thousand soldiers marched behind Lincoln's ornate catafalque, and seventy-five thousand civilians joined them. The entire population was thrown into a veritable paroxysm of grief, with a single exception. One small six year-old lad was so perplexed by the sorrow he saw in his mother's face that he couldn't shed a tear.

Although the boy's father was from New York, sympathy for the South during the Civil War held sway in his home because of his mother who hailed from Georgia. She was a true southern belle whose family had owned slaves, and whose two brothers had fought for the Confederacy.

In the last stages of the war, the young boy had faint memories of the "care packages" of medicine and supplies his mother sent surreptitiously to the South. So strong were her southern sympathies that his father refused to fight against the Confederates, although he lent moral support to the Union cause.

Therefore on that last Tuesday in April 1865, the six year-old just did not understand why he and his brother were being made to stand there by the window on the second floor of his Broadway home and watch the body of Abraham Lincoln go by. After all, the President had been the one who ordered General Sherman to march to the sea and in the process take his Grandfather Bulloch's plantation. Yet there they were watching reverently as Lincoln's cortege made its way to Union Square.

The boy turned from his parents and leaned his head out of the window for a better look. What he saw resembled a circus, except that no one was laughing. A squad of mounted police took the lead. Then came a hundred dragoons with black and white plumes and red, yellow, and blue facings on their uniforms. After that came that terrible coffin. He imagined what its contents must look like.

After what must have seemed like an eternity, the parade was finally over, and his life returned to normal. Over the years, his recollections of April 25, 1865, faded into the inner folds of his memory until September 14, 1901. On that day, another United States President died from an assassin's bullet, and it all came rushing back.

You see, with the death of William McKinley, Vice-President Theodore Roosevelt, that little fellow in the New York window, suddenly became President. In a tragic twist in time, he finally understood that sorrow could sometimes grip an entire nation regardless of political persuasion.

DEVOTION PAYS DIVIDENDS

Lucretia Garfield

    Lucretia Rudolph was born of humble origins in 1832. Her father was an Ohio carpenter who just barely kept the wolf from the door. At the age of eighteen, she made good her escape from her meager existence at home and enrolled in the Western Reserve Eclectic Institute in Hiram, Ohio. There she met the man who would one day become her husband and eventually rescue her from the threat of poverty—that perennial dread which gnawed at the innards of most every woman in the 19th century. Unfortunately, it took the patience of Job on her part as well as his death at the hands of an assassin to give her that much sought for peace of mind that financial security could bring.
    Lucretia and her beau became engaged in 1854 and became husband and wife four years later. During that time, she was a faithful, duty-bound spouse, even in the face of her husband's blatant womanizing.

First there was Rebecca Selleck, and then came Kate Chase, the daughter of Salmon P. Chase, U.S. Secretary of the Treasury. Lucretia stoically withstood their assaults on her domestic tranquility. After all, what was a poor woman to do?

In 1863, Lucretia's husband was elected to Congress, and they went to Washington, D.C. She never became part of the social scene of the nation's capital, but he availed himself of every opportunity to make new friends, especially women. Lucretia bore it all with dignity, but Washington's insiders buzzed with titillation over her husband's dalliances.

Finally, the Congressman went one step too far. One of his tête-à-têtes turned serious. He met and engaged in an ongoing relationship with one Lucia Gilbert Calhoun, a New York newspaper reporter. When Lucretia's husband apprised her of his love for Lucia, his confession shook his wife's world, and she put her foot down firmly enough to force a breakup of the affair. As far as the record shows, this was the end of her husband's roving. That took care of one problem.

Shortly thereafter, the political star of Lucretia's husband began to rise in the Republican Party, and he moved up to a leadership position in the House. When he was later elected to the United States Senate and then to the Presidency, it appeared that Lucretia's financial worries were over. She was apparently headed for easy street, and that would solve problem number two.

Then came that fateful day in 1881, Lucretia and her husband had occupied the White House for just four months when he was shot by a disgruntled job seeker. Although Lucretia had just recovered from a bout with malaria, she maintained a vigil of more than two months at her husband's side. The country was awe-struck as it watched President James A. Garfield's wife stand by him in death just as she had in life.

The President's demise, of course, created a problem for Lucretia. How could she now support herself? Was she to live for the rest of her life with one or more of her children?

Had she escaped the poverty of her childhood only to become impecunious once again—this time at the age of fifty? The nation thought not!

You see, Lucretia's selfless devotion to her husband through thick and thin pulled at the heartstrings of the people. In a generous twist in time, somebody started a campaign to raise money for her. That netted the President's widow $360,000! Then Congress appropriated $50,000 to help ameliorate her grief and voted her an annual pension of $5,000 on top of that.

Lucretia lived another thirty-seven years. She took her money and moved to sunny Pasadena, California, where at the age of eighty-five, she died a most contented woman. In the end her persistence paid off, and her devotion returned dividends.

FIGHTING JOE WHEELER
SERVED TWO MASTERS

When the Battleship Maine mysteriously exploded in Havana Harbor on February 15, 1898, America's battle cry became "Remember the Maine! To Hell with Spain!" The United States quickly went to war against the moribund Spanish Empire, and President William McKinley placed Congressman Joe Wheeler in charge of the nation's volunteer forces. The Commander-in-Chief made Wheeler a two-star general, but in so doing, he set the stage for a vigorous debate eight years later. After his death in 1906, they buried Wheeler in Arlington National Cemetery, but not without considerable controversy over the General's burial clothes.

After the outbreak of the Spanish-American War, General Wheeler took command of a largely unmounted cavalry division in William R. Shafter's V Corps. The troops under his command, which included Theodore Roosevelt's "Rough Riders," won the Battle of Las Guasimas and took part in the assault on San Juan Heights near Santiago, Cuba.

At the conclusion of the campaign in Cuba, General Wheeler commanded a brigade in the Philippines, and after the war he was placed in charge of the convalescent camp at Montauk Point, New York. Subsequently, Wheeler commanded the Department of the Lakes until his retirement in September 1900.

For the next five years, Wheeler toured the country speaking on military affairs and assisting in various civic projects. In 1906, he went to visit a sister in Brooklyn, New York, and on January 25, he died unexpectedly.

Wheeler's son, Major Joseph Wheeler, Jr., then announced that his father was going to be honored for his service in the Spanish-American

WWW.TwistInTime.COM

War by being laid to rest in Arlington National Cemetery. The authorities had given their assent, but this was before they learned what the younger Wheeler had in mind.

They had been told by the son that his father would be buried in his Major General's outfit, and they assumed the two stars would be on the shoulder straps of the deceased's United States Army uniform. The younger Wheeler, however, had something else in mind. He wanted his father buried in his Major General's uniform all right, but not that of the United States!

After several attempts to dissuade the younger Wheeler, the officials of Arlington finally gave in, since they had already given permission for Wheeler's interment in Arlington. Hence they buried General "Fighting Joe" Wheeler in a Major General's uniform, but it was gray instead of blue!

For you see, before old "Fighting Joe" Wheeler put on the Union blue to serve in the Spanish-American War, he had rendered vigorous service as a Major General in the army of the Confederate States of America. When President William McKinley made the old soldier a Major General for the second time and sent him to fight in Cuba, he did so on the basis of Wheeler's reputation for winning battles against the United States during the Civil War.

Thus in a strange twist in time, today Joseph Wheeler is the only General buried in Arlington National Cemetery wearing the uniform of the Confederacy. He had worn a pair of stars for both the Blue and the Gray and had fought for each in two different wars. In the end, however, the Gray won out. Apparently some things are just not susceptible to change.

ONE SOLDIER'S LEGACY
FROM MISSIONARY RIDGE

General Arthur MacArthur

On September 5, 1912, in Milwaukee, Wisconsin, 90 aged Civil War Veterans gathered for their annual reunion. Seated at the head table was their leader, now a retired Lieutenant General, and behind him was the flag that had propelled him to rapid advancement and the Congressional Medal of Honor. Before the night was over, however, in a moment of choking irony, the General would suddenly leave the hall with that flag, much to the chagrin of everyone assembled.

They had all been with the General on that November day back in 1863. At the time he held the rank of First Lieutenant. The old soldiers remembered how they had all charged behind him up Missionary Ridge above Chattanooga, Tennessee, as he waved the flag in triumph. Twice he had retrieved it after its carriers were killed, and as he held the battered and scarred banner aloft at the top of the ridge, he yelled, "On Wisconsin!" Hundreds followed him to an improbable victory.

When Brigadier General Philip A. Sheridan reached the summit of Missionary Ridge that evening, he embraced the young, teen-aged officer and told his men, "Take care of him. He has just won the Medal of Honor." Well, take care of him they did. They elected him Major, and four months later he was brevetted again, this time to Colonel, the youngest of that rank in the entire Union Army.

When the war was over, he stayed in the military and rose in rank. In 1909, he retired with three stars, and now three years later he was going to meet with his old comrades in arms.

The hall became deathly quiet, and as he stepped to the speaker's rostrum he looked up at that same battered and torn flag he had carried up Missionary Ridge. Then he turned to look at what was left of the 24th Wisconsin. He started to speak but never finished his sentence.

"Your indomitable regiment...," was all he managed to say before he collapsed on the floor. Dr. William Cronyn, the regimental surgeon, reached him first. He quickly examined the General and then shouted that he was dying. The men gathered around their fallen hero and said the Lord's Prayer. By the time they finished, he was dead.

According to the minutes of that emotional meeting, Captain Edwin Parsons rose to his feet, took the flag off the wall and wrapped it around their leader. Then they carried him out.

The General had often said that he had wanted to die at the head of his regiment, but who could have imagined that it would have been accomplished in such a fitting fashion? Who could have dreamed that the very flag he carried so valiantly at Missionary Ridge would enwrap his body nearly fifty years later, as they carried him out of the building at the head of what was left of the 24th Wisconsin? Finally, who could have guessed that his own son would then carry on his tradition of heroism?

For you see, among the crowd of mourners on the day they laid the General to rest was a Captain who would one day follow his father into the military hall of fame. In an ironic twist in time, General Arthur MacArthur had set the bar of bravery for his own son, General Douglas MacArthur, on those heights of Missionary Ridge.

THE BULL RUN
"RUNNERS"

The festivities began early one July morning in 1861. Large numbers of Washington's most important people were packing their picnic baskets and making ready for the ride to Bull Run. They were sure the Union Army would rout the Rebels that day, and they all wanted to be there to witness it, especially Henry Wilson.

Henry had worked hard to reach the social station he now occupied. After serving his apprenticeship as a cobbler in Natick, Massachusetts, he worked himself into the position of a successful shoe manufacturer. That's how he got into politics, and that's why he was on the road to Bull Run on July 21, 1861.

The road was crowded that day. Servants driving luxurious carriages loaded with husbands, wives, daughters and sweethearts, vied for the right of way, but Henry held his own. He and his lady had their hamper filled with champagne with which they intended to toast the Union victory before they marched on to Richmond for the coup d'e tat.

However, when the two armies met in that first real battle of the Civil War, things didn't quite go as Henry Wilson and the Northern Generals had planned. The Rebels were reinforced by Johnson and Jackson, and soon the "splendid" Federal army had turned and was frantically flying back toward Washington, allowing nothing to get in its way.

All along the line of retreat, confusion reigned. The Union troops and their civilian cheerleaders became one panic-stricken mob. The ladies' shattered trunks filled with ball dresses, which they had planned to wear that night in Richmond, lay strewn along the way. Gossamer robes were trampled under the feet of men and horses. Huge baskets of wine and all kinds of other delicacies marked the line of retreat. It was total chaos, and Henry Wilson was right in the middle of it—on foot.

He had been separated from his lady and his carriage, and he found himself desperately looking for a ride back to the capital. That's when he spied a soldier and a wagon.

Battle of Bull Run

Henry stumbled along side the teamster and begged to be allowed to climb aboard. The soldier repeatedly refused the request and whipped his mules on down the road, leaving Henry to get to Washington the best way he could.

Perhaps if the teamster had known whom it was that he was leaving in the dust, Henry would have had an easier time getting home, but then how was the soldier to know? You see, United States Senators didn't wear badges of rank, and there was certainly no way he could have known that Senator Henry Wilson would become the Vice-President of the United States after the war.

On second thought, however, given the trauma of the day, one suspects that the soldier might have lashed his mules on down the road anyway. In a hectic twist in time, rank would have to wait awhile for its privileges in the mad rush back to the nation's capital after the First Battle of Bull Run.

TOO MANY PIGS
FOR THE TEATS

President Abraham Lincoln

In the winter of 1864, a corporal who had just been discharged after serving for three years in the Union Army made application for the sutlership at Point Island Federal Prison in Maryland. As a civilian, he could now get his share of the money being handed out to those who made a living selling supplies to the military.

To secure this position, the young entrepreneur made application to Secretary of War Stanton, and when he was turned down, he decided to appeal to Abraham Lincoln. After all, everybody knew that Lincoln was close to the people. He had a backwoods, homespun way about him that set people at ease. Little did the corporal know just how backwoods and homespun Lincoln could be. At times, he was downright earthy.

Edwin Station's response to the corporal's application was typically cavalier. He eyed the lad and then summarily denied his request. "I think we can give this position to a soldier who has lost an arm or a leg. He would be more deserving." Then without allowing any further discussion, Stanton dismissed the applicant with a wave of the hand. That's when the corporal decided to go see the President.

WWW.TWISTINTIME.COM

In those days, even with the war, personal access to the President by the common citizen was freely given. The corporal went to Lincoln's office and was ushered into the room. The young man began to make his plea, and Lincoln sat listening almost imperiously. It was as if he was having an audience with the Pope or the King of England. Where was the President's ease of manner? Where was his down home style? Where was the comic relief of his cracker-barrel wit? Was all of that a myth? It certainly seemed as much. The Abraham Lincoln, before whom he now stood, reminded him of the stiff and unyielding Stanton.

Upon the completion of his personal appeal, Lincoln asked him a single question. "Have you seen Mr. Stanton?" When the corporal said that he had, Lincoln replied, "I am sorry; I can't help you. This is Mr. Stanton's business."

The corporal paid his respects and turned for the door. He was stunned. This was not the man he had expected to meet. This was not the people's president. This was a carbon copy of Edwin Stanton.

Then he heard the President clear his throat and call him back. As he turned to face Lincoln again, he saw a different man. He sat relaxed, and his face wore a sympathetic look. Here was the down-home demeanor that the corporal had expected, and the President's words matched that image.

"Young man," Lincoln said softly. "I have thousands of applications like this every day, but we cannot satisfy them all. These positions are just like office seekers—there are just too many pigs for the teats."

The ladies who were listening to the conversation placed their handkerchiefs to their faces and turned away, but the President's words put the corporal in a good humor. You see, his confidence in Abraham Lincoln was restored. Surely he was the greatest man to ever fill the Presidential chair. In a relaxing twist in time, Lincoln revealed that he was the people's President, even if he was a little bit earthy from time to time.

THE KILLER RETURNED TO THE SCENE OF THE CRIME

John Wilkes Booth

The events of April 14, 1865, at Ford's Theatre in Washington, D.C. have become a familiar part of our nation's history. It was there that John Wilkes Booth shot Abraham Lincoln in the head while the President and his wife were watching a performance of "Our American Cousin." It is a well-known fact that Booth was able to escape from the theatre that night, only to be killed a few days later. What is not so commonly known is that after his death a part of Booth came back to haunt Ford's Theatre for years.

After the assassination, it didn't take his co-conspirators long to realize that there was no chance to escape, so they surrendered. For Booth, however, it was another story. The day before, he had penned in his diary, "I have too great a soul to die a criminal…let me die bravely." Thus it was that Booth remained in his hiding place even after the barn in which he had taken refuge was set on fire.

Silhouetted by the flames, Booth stepped closer to the door. Balancing himself on a crutch he peered through the slats, and that is when Sergeant Boston Corbett broke his orders to bring the assassin back alive and instead shot Booth.

Lincoln's killer was dragged to the porch of the Garrett farmhouse where he lay for two hours before he died. At 8:30 A.M. on Wednesday, April 26, 1865, Booth's body was then taken to the Potomac River and placed on board the Montauk, where an autopsy was performed. The body was laid out on a carpenter's bench, which served as an improvised bier.

The bullet that killed John Wilkes Booth struck him near the base of the skull and shattered several vertebrae. These were removed from the body, which was then placed in a makeshift coffin and buried in Washington's Old Penitentiary. The assassin would remain in that grave for four years, until, after continued pleas by Edwin Booth and his mother, President Andrew Johnson allowed them to have the body and bury it in an unmarked grave in the family plot at Baltimore. Meanwhile, a strange series of events created a reunion of sorts back at Ford's Theatre.

After the assassination, the theatre was never opened for performances again. It was purchased by the government from John Ford, its owner, and for a time was used as a storehouse for Confederate records. Then it was turned into an Army Medical Museum, and that's when the irony concerning John Wilkes Booth turned thick.

You see, parts of his remains were returned to the scene of his crime. His shattered vertebrae, which had been removed during the autopsy, were put on display almost within the shadow of the presidential box in which he shot the President.

In a macabre twist in time, after the shooting Abraham Lincoln was carried away from the scene of the tragedy and died, while John Wilkes Booth died and was brought back. The victim left, and the perpetrator stayed. History apparently has its own way of getting even.

THE LUCK OF THE IRISH

General Thomas Francis Meagher was Irish through and through. His unbridled love for Ireland got him in trouble with the British in his native land, so he came to America. Here he put his life on the line for the Union during the Civil War, but just after the fighting ended, his courage finally cost him his life.

Meagher was born in Waterford, Ireland, and grew up to be one of the leaders of the "Young Ireland Party." When he immigrated to the United States, he settled in New York City and became active in the Irish independence movement there.

Thomas Francis Meagher

Then came the War Between the States, and he joined the army as a Major in charge of an Irish Zouave Company. By 1862, he had made it all the way to Brigadier General and commanded the 2nd Irish Brigade.

Meagher made a fearless leader for the already pugilistic Irish soldiers. He first attracted attention at the Battle of First Bull Run and Seven Pines. At Antietam he had a horse shot out from under him. It took him only a moment to recover, and when he got to his feet, he began waving his sword at the green Irish guideon, shouting "Look at that flag and remember Ireland." His boys didn't let him down.

After Antietam, however, came Fredericksburg where despite his courage, his unit was decimated. They took what was left of the Irish Brigade and distributed them among other units, giving Meagher a minor command in the West, which he held until the end of the war.

Then in 1865, his adopted country called on him for service again. His fortitude and leadership skills won him the position of Territorial Governor of Montana, so Meagher heeded the call and headed west with an idea for populating the territory.

Once he had been sworn in as governor, he announced that he was going to make a trip to New York to meet with his Irish friends and convince them to help him create new settlements out of the hordes of Irish who were trying to establish themselves in America.

That all sounded well and good to everybody except those who opposed Irish immigration. You see, among the chief opponents to Meagher's plan was the American "Know Nothing Party." They were against any newcomers to America, so when the Governor set out in the summer of 1867 for New York, the Know Nothings hatched their plot.

In a treacherous twist in time, on the evening of July 1, 1867, Meagher was alone on the deck of an eastbound riverboat. Somehow, with the steamer near Benton, Montana, he mysteriously fell over board and drowned in the Missouri River.

Thus this daredevil who had once been sentenced to be drawn and quartered in Ireland, this fearless warrior who survived every attempt by the Confederates to kill him, died an ignominious death in the muddy waters of the Missouri River trying to find a better life for his countrymen. Small wonder they are called the "Fighting Irish!"

TEXANS WHO COULD NOT BE THROTTLED

Like every other commander in the Civil War, Confederate General Joseph E. Johnston was a stickler for following orders, especially in the heat of battle. When he sent out a tactical directive, he expected it to be followed to the letter. If it wasn't, he would go into paroxysms of madness, except for that time in 1862, when a contingent of Texans misunderstood their orders and put a smile on the General's face.

Immediately after the battle of Williamsburg on May 5, 1862, Johnston received word that Union forces had ventured up the York River a bit and landed. By all accounts the Yankees were ravaging the countryside under the protection of their gun-boats on the river.

General Johnston sent a message to one of his brigade commanders, General John B. Hood, ordering him to check the enemy's advance by "feeling him gently and then falling back to avoid an engagement." Johnston calculated that this would draw the Union soldiers away from the protection of their gunboats. If he could just lure them a few miles from the river, he could outflank and capture them all.

After receiving Johnston's orders, Hood gave the

assignment to a contingent from Texas who was "spoiling for a fight." Like a horse with the bit between his teeth, they went after the Yankees with complete abandon, and once they were in battle, they forgot all about their "feel and fall back" directive. Once they had the enemy on the run. The Texans couldn't help themselves. They chased them almost to the river's bank, killing and capturing several hundred.

At first, Johnston was angry. He commanded a conference with Hood and demanded to know why his orders were not obeyed.

"General Hood," Johnston asked, "Have you given me an illustration of the Texas idea of 'feeling an enemy gently and falling back? If so, what would your Texans have done, sir, if I had ordered them to charge and drive the enemy?"

Hood replied, "I suppose, General, they would have driven them into the river and tried to swim out and capture the gun-boats."

After that explanation, General Johnston admonished General Hood to "Teach your Texans that the first duty of a soldier is literally to obey orders."

Hood saluted and assured his commander that his men would obey every jot and tittle of all future orders. He then turned his horse back toward his troops, somewhat deflated that General Johnston never took cognizance of the grit his Texans had shown in the face of overwhelming odds.

What Hood could not have seen, however, was the smile on General Johnston's face as he rode toward his headquarters, conversing with his aide-de-camp. In the future, Johnston mumbled almost to himself, he would take into account when he sent Texans into battle.

You see, descendants of those men who cried "Remember the Alamo," a generation earlier, would find it extremely difficult to ever treat the enemy "gently," nor could they ever find it easy to "draw back."

Perhaps that's why, in a determined twist in time, the last Confederate soldiers to lay down their arms were from Texas.

THE THIRD TIME HAD NO CHARM

George S. Patton

    The young Confederate army officer felt the impact of the minie ball as it tore through his body and knocked him off his horse. With the bone in his upper right arm shattered, he tried to escape but could not move quickly enough. At a place called Scary Creek in western Virginia, he was captured by Yankee soldiers. It is too bad they didn't keep him; he might have survived the war, but then his grandson and namesake would have been deprived of a hero he could emulate in a later conflict.

    Within a short time after his capture, the young man was paroled, and in less than a year he was in the thick of battle again. In May of 1862, while serving as a Lieutenant Colonel under General Wharton, he was struck with a minie ball for the second time. This one hit him in the stomach, and was thought certainly to be mortal.

    As the wounded officer lay on his cot awaiting death, General Wharton rode by and inquired about his condition. The younger man replied that he had been told that it would be fatal but that he did not feel like a dead man. Wharton dismounted, knelt by his side, and asked if he could examine the wound.

General Wharton stuck his unwashed finger in and felt around. Suddenly he hit something hard and exclaimed, "What is this?" Fishing around a bit more, he pulled out a ten-dollar gold piece. The bullet had struck the coin and pushed it into the man's flesh and then glanced off. Thus did the young Lieutenant Colonel escape death once more, and after a period of convalescence, he was on the battlefield again.

By the summer of 1864, the young officer, who was now a Colonel and commanded his own brigade, served under General Jubal Early. On September 19, his unit went up against General Philip Sheridan's Army of the Shenandoah in the Third Battle of Winchester. It was a ferocious fight in which the young Colonel's brigade was crushed while attempting to defend the left flank. In the process, he was mortally wounded.

They took him to a nearby farm house where for six days he struggled to survive. On September 25, 1864, he lost the fight for his life, and they buried the 31 year-old Colonel at Winchester.

Through the years, his reputation grew, as did those of his six brothers who served with him in the Confederate Army. You see, they were a fighting family--always had been and always would be. His grandson proved that.

In an ironic twist in time, when General George S. Patton armed with his ivory-handled pistols led two separate armies against the Nazis, he often reflected on his grandfather, the first George S. Patton, who after being shot three times finally gave up his life in battle. Some family traditions just don't change.

THE WEEK NEW YORK WENT CRAZY

New York Draft Riots

It was 4:00 in the afternoon on July 13, 1863. With the Union victories at Vicksburg and Gettysburg, the corner had been turned in the Civil War. The North had every reason to celebrate, but in New York City an inexplicable rage boiled to the surface. Whites took to the streets in droves in search of Black residents.

Inside the New York City Colored Orphan Asylum, 233 children were studying, playing in the nursery, or lying on a sick bed in the dispensary. None of them had any idea of the horror that was about to descend upon them. Just outside, several thousand angry white men, women, and children, armed with clubs, brickbats etc. made ready to give vent to their uncontrollable anger.

The mob had begun its rampage earlier in the day when it attacked a Black fruit vendor and his nine-year-old helper. Now as it prepared to invade the four-story home of the Black orphans, the caretakers quickly escorted the terrified children out the side entrances and hurried them to the nearest police station. When one White bystander shouted support for the children, the rioters turned on him, and he barely escaped with his life.

From the orphanage for Blacks, the mob burned the home of abolitionist Abby Hopper Gibbons and then headed for the waterfront. At the docks, they attacked William Jones, a black longshoreman, hanged him, and then burned his body. From that point, there was no stopping the rampaging crowd.

Although both Black men and women were attacked, the rioters singled out the men. One group jumped a black sailor, plunged a knife into him and smashed his body with stones. Another part of the mob caught a black coachman, Abraham Franklin, and hanged him from a lamppost as they cheered for Jefferson Davis, the Confederate President! Then they dragged his body through the streets.

The crowds were pitiless. After James Costello shot at and fled from a white attacker, six men beat, stomped, kicked, and stoned him before hanging him.

The mayhem continued for five days, and during that time the rioters lynched 11 Black men and forced hundreds of other Blacks out of the city. Almost over night, New York City became a White domain, as the Black population plummeted to its lowest point since 1820.

Oddly enough, this ugly episode in American history is known as the "Draft Riots." Ostensibly the rioters were protesting the Conscription Act, but there was a deeper and more ominous reason for their anger. It was really President Lincoln who set off that angry, deadly mob. The imposition of the draft was only the spark that ignited the conflagration.

You see, when the Emancipation Proclamation took effect on January 1, 1863, only a handful of Whites in New

York supported it. Then when the draft law was enacted in March, the city's Copperheads (for the most part Democrats) began to inflame public opinion. They insisted that the war to preserve the Union had been turned into a conflict to free the slaves, and that's when the anger began to build.

In a revealing twist in time, when that New York mob hit the streets in July 1863, Blacks became the object of their wrath, not the government, and that's how the rioters showed their true colors. They would fight for the Union, but not to end slavery. They were determined to keep the Black man in his place.

POLITICAL RIVALRY WITH LINCOLN LASTED TO THE END

Salmon Chase

Salmon Chase was never a friend of Abraham Lincoln's, although he served as his Secretary of the Treasury from 1861 to 1864. So complete was his political disloyalty to the President that no one was surprised at Chase's behavior on the day that Lincoln died. They rightly assumed that his cold-hearted reaction stemmed from his dislike of the man who stole the Presidency from him in 1860.

By the time that John Wilkes Booth committed his dastardly deed in 1865, Salmon Chase was no longer in Lincoln's cabinet. Over his three and one-half year tenure as head of the Treasury Department, Chase had tweaked the President's nose with threats to quit just one time too many. The fourth threat broke the camel's back, and Lincoln surprised Chase by accepting his resignation. Lincoln then put his rival on a political shelf by naming him Chief Justice of the United States Supreme Court. Chase swallowed his pride and accepted the proffered judicial position, but he was never happy there.

On April 14, 1865, as the mortally wounded President was carried from Ford's theater across Tenth Street to a room in the Petersen boarding house, Lincoln's cabinet and other important government officials gathered at the President's side—all but Salmon P. Chase. He was in bed and when awakened with the news, he simply informed the messenger that he "could do no good and would probably be in the way." With that he returned to his slumbers.

The next morning Chase got up early, dressed, and headed toward the Petersen House. At last the Chief Justice was coming to join the nation's leaders in their deathwatch, or so everyone thought. As Chase reached the boarding house, he was told that the President was still barely alive. Without showing any emotion, he just kept right on walking. The crowd, which had gathered at the steps, could not believe their eyes. Chase was not going to pay his respects to Abraham Lincoln, not even in his dying hour.

Maunsell B. Field, the man whom Chase had wanted to be his Assistant Treasury Secretary ran after him and gave him a full account of the tragedy. Chase continued without missing a beat; he just kept walking. Finally, the Chief Justice reached the Kirkwood House and stopped. There he stood and waited until news was brought to him that the President had died, and it was then that he made his move.

Inside the Kirkwood House was Andrew Johnson, who was waiting to be sworn in by Chase as the nation's 17th President. Chief Justice Chase quickly administered the oath of office and then returned to his own home without ever visiting Lincoln that day.

Official Washington tried to cover up Chase's absence with renderings of drawings showing the Chief Justice at Lincoln's bedside, but it was just wishful thinking. He had done his duty to the President at the Kirkwood House. As for Lincoln, as Secretary of War Stanton had said, "Now he belongs to the ages," and that was all right with Salmon P. Chase.

TRIFLING WITH OLD GLORY

General Benjamin Butler

    The flag of the United States has been the subject of considerable controversy throughout American history. Malcontents have often claimed the right to burn the flag, spit on the flag, or stomp the flag, all in the name of free speech. Although there have been several legislative attempts to protect the stars and stripes from such outrages, for the most part these efforts have been futile. Today just about anybody can do whatever he or she wants to do to Old Glory and get away with it, but it hasn't always been that way. There once was a time when dishonoring the American flag could get a fellow in deep trouble, as the case of William Mumford amply illustrates.

    William B. Mumford was a native of North Carolina who as an adult was lured to the gambling tables of New Orleans to earn his living as a professional card player. Mumford soon built a reputation for being foolhardy and reckless in games of chance. That's why no one was surprised when he attacked the United States flag at the top of the New Orleans Mint.

It was in April of 1862, when the Union navy captured New Orleans and raised the Union flag over the mint. It had only been there for a short time when a number of locals, including William Mumford, decided to haul it down. With cheers from the onlookers, Mumford started out to carry the despised emblem to the mayor at city hall, but before he could reach his destination, angry citizens of New Orleans grabbed at it as he was walking. By the time Mumford reached the mayor, the flag had been torn to shreds.

Now it just so happened that Major General Benjamin Butler, commander of the Union ground forces heard about the incident and decided that the flag of the United States was not going to become the subject of such vile treatment—not on his watch—so he had Mumford arrested.

At first Mumford treated the whole matter lightly until he was given a copy of General Order Number 70. That was when he found out just how serious the Yankees were about the flag. For you see, the special order, issued by Butler announced that Mumford would pay for his act of disrespect with his life.

In a strange twist in time, on June 7, 1862, the army took William Mumford back to the courtyard of the mint—the place where he hauled down the flag in the first place and hanged him.

Ironically, waving majestically in the breeze above the gallows that day was the emblem that cost Mumford his life. Obviously there once was a time when disrespect of the American flag was hazardous to one's health.

NO MERCY FOR MARY SURRATT

The four condemned conspirators, one woman and three men, climbed up the 13 steps of the scaffold at 11:00 on the morning of July 7th, 1865. They had been convicted and sentenced to death for the assassination of President Abraham Lincoln. Within minutes they were all dangling lifelessly from the end of a rope. Shortly thereafter, the nation breathed a collective sigh of relief, never dreaming that a government official had treacherously arranged the death of one of them, Mrs. Mary E. Surratt.

Secretary of War, Edwin Stanton, had named Judge Advocate General Joseph Holt to conduct the trial of the eight prisoners who had been charged with conspiring to kill the President. The proceedings, which began on May 9th, ended 50 days later when a military commission found four of them guilty and sentenced them to death by hanging. All that remained was for President Andrew Johnson to sign the order.

As fate would have it, the President was ill at the time, so Judge Advocate General Holt had to wait until July fifth before he could get Johnson to review the sentences and sign the execution order.

When Holt was finally able to give the documents to the President, Johnson preferred not to wade through all of the findings of the commission. He simply asked that they be summarized for him. Judge Holt complied, with one exception. He made no mention of a special request from the military tribunal concerning Mrs. Surratt that would have saved her from becoming the first woman in the history of the United States to be legally executed!

You see, after the defendants had been found guilty and the commission met to decide their punishment, they voted for the death penalty for all four. However, on the last page of their findings, they attached a recommendation for mercy for Mrs. Surratt. Citing her age and gender, the commission urged the President to extend mercy to her and commute her sentence to life imprisonment. Holt deviously withheld this document from the President.

BILL COATE

Johnson signed the execution order, without ever seeing the recommendation for mercy, and on July 7th, 1865, Mary climbed those gallows steps followed by her co-defendants, George Atzerodt, David E. Herold, and Lewis Paine.

On that fateful morning Mary E. Surratt had a 20-strand rope, one and a half inches in circumference, placed around her neck and then a hood pulled over her head. In a few moments she was dead—not necessarily because she was guilty—but because the jury's recommendation for mercy never reached the President's hand. In a guileful twist in time, the judge sealed Mary's fate by subterfuge. Apparently the temper of the times forced honorable men to commit dishonorable acts, all in the name of satisfying a widespread thirst for revenge.

Mary Surratt

WILD WEST ODDITIES
WITH A TWIST

THE TEN COMMANDMENTS OF STAGE COACH TRAVEL

The Stagecoach that took Horace Greeley West

On May 9, 1859, the influential editor of a widely circulated eastern newspaper decided to come west via stagecoach. His journey was about to become one of the most famous trips in American journalism. Carpetbag and umbrella in hand, he looked forward to escaping the restraints of civilization. Little did he know just how circumscribed his overland trip would be.

The Eastern newspaperman soon found out that traveling in a stagecoach was an unforgettable experience, even for the high and mighty. Not only did one have to contend with odors, dust, and highwaymen; there were those ubiquitous posters that hung in every Butterfield stage stop reminding him of the Ten Commandments for riding the stages.

"Abstinence from liquor is preferred," read rule number one. "If you must drink, however, share the bottle, and don't overlook the driver."

"If ladies are present, gentlemen are urged to forgo smoking cigars and pipes, as the odor of same is repugnant. Chewing tobacco is permitted, if you spit with the wind, and not against it."

"Gentlemen passengers must refrain from the use of rough language in the presence of ladies and children. This rule does not apply to the driver, whose team may not be able to understand genteel language."

"Robes are provided for your comfort during cold or wet weather. Hogging robes will not be tolerated. The offender will be obliged to ride outside with the driver."

"Snoring is disgusting. If you sleep, sleep quietly."

"Don't use your fellow passenger's shoulder for a pillow. He or she may not understand, and friction could result."

"Do not discharge firearms for pleasure or shoot at wild animals along the roadsides. The noise riles the horses."

"In the event of a runaway, don't jump from the coach. It may leave you injured or at the mercy of the highwaymen and coyotes."

"Topics of discussion to be avoided have to do with religion, politics, and above all, stagecoach robbery and accidents."

"Gentlemen guilty of unchivalrous behavior toward lady passengers will be put off the stage. It is a long walk back to the station. A word to the wise is sufficient."

Thus did the man who coined the phrase, "Go West Young Man, Go West," follow his own advice, for you see, that eastern newspaperman was none other than Horace Greeley, editor of the New York Tribune. It is interesting to note, however, that he didn't stay. In a prudent twist in time, when he made his return to the east, he took a ship. He apparently had had enough of those binding stagecoach rules.

FRONTIER JUSTICE
WAS SWIFT AND SURE

Most of the argonauts who were drawn west by the California gold rush were decent people who were simply trying to seize an opportunity. There was a minority, however, who showed a lawless streak—the rogues—those ne'er-do-wells who preyed on their fellow miners. They did so, however, at great risk. The law-abiding folks in California would brook no nonsense, and they never forgot.

On January 18, 1849, four men stumbled into a lean-to saloon that had been slapped together by two Frenchmen at Dry Diggings, not far from Coloma. They drank and gambled so late into the night that the proprietors went to bed leaving their guests to their revelry.

Sometime later, the drunken quartet decided to rob the saloonkeepers and took off with $600.

The victims immediately sounded the alarm and by dawn a huge posse of miners was hot on the trail of the thieves. By nightfall, they had the robbers in custody. On the next day the miners held a trial and found the four men guilty. On January 21st, they were tied to a tree and each given 39 lashes, after which they were banned from the mining district.

The foursome had no sooner been sent along their way than word came that they had earlier committed two murders at nearby Weaver's Creek. Quickly another tribunal was held, and the perpetrators were tried in absentia. Death was decreed, and once more a posse was formed.

On January 24, 1849, three of the four fugitives were caught, and on January 25, they were hanged. In a swift twist in time, just six days had elapsed since they had robbed the saloonkeepers and five days since their flogging. In less than one week, they had committed one crime, been tried twice, whipped once, and then hanged. No one could say that those California gold miners didn't tend to business when it came to dealing with the scum of the countryside.

BILL COATE

HOW SAMUEL CLEMENS PICKED MARK TWAIN

We all know that the man who created Tom Sawyer, Becky Thatcher, and Huckleberry Finn, was born into this world as Samuel Clemens. When he began to write for the public, he tried a number of pen names, one of which was the awkward "Sieur Louis de Conte." Thankfully, he later settled on Mark Twain. That part is a common story and often told. What is not so well known, however, is how Clemens came up with the pseudonym by which the world came to know him.

Samuel Clemens loved the paddlewheel steamboats, and he loved the river. In the late 1850s, he got a job on a Mississippi River boat as a leadsman. His task was to keep the pilot apprised of the depth of the water, and that experience later gave him his pen name.

As leadsman, Clemens had to stand on the bow of the boat with a 30 foot-long line attached to a pipe. The line had markings woven into its strands, which represented various depths. His job was to heave the line out, let the pipe sink to the bottom, and then yell out the depth. The process was called "heaving the lead" and "singing the mark," and Clemens was good at it.

If Clemens threw out the lead and the water reached the first strip of leather on the line, he would holler out, "Mark One!" That meant that the water was six feet deep. If the pilot heard him yell, "Quarter One," he knew the depth was 7 1/2 feet. Likewise, "Half One" signaled 9 feet of water. "Quarter less Twain" meant a depth of 10 ½ feet, and Quarter Twain indicated a depth of 13 ½ feet of water.

Riverboat pilots listened very carefully for the leadsman's song, and when that special call which signaled a 12 feet depth was heard, the pilot smiled with gladness, for he knew he was in "safe water."

We all know Samuel Clemens eventually left the river, but he never forgot it. You see, when he began to cast about for a pen name, his mind went back to those halcyon days on the Mississippi River when he "heaved the lead" and "sang the mark." He remembered the call that signaled "safe water" and decided to use that as his pen name. What could have been more appropriate for a riverboat man turned writer?

So in a propitious twist in time, Samuel Clemens chose the leadsman's call, "Mark Twain," as his pen name. To everybody on a riverboat, it meant they were steaming in 12 feet of water, and they were safe. For Samuel Clemens, the "safe water" call meant he was in safe literary waters, and he was reminded of this every time he signed his name, "Mark Twain."

Mark Twain

INSIDER INFORMATION AT THE CONSTITUTIONAL CONVENTION

Colton Hall

Benjamin S. Lippincott was definitely "one of the boys;" at least that's how historian H.H. Bancroft described him. He also called Lippincott a gambler. Now it may be true that Lippincott was well connected, but to suggest that he was a gambler seems to go a bit far. Old Ben was never cavalier with a coin. He always knew what he was doing in financial matters.

Lippincott came to California from New York in that huge covered wagon migration of 1846. Upon his arrival at Sutter's Fort, he joined John C. Fremont's California Battalion and fought in the Mexican-American war. After the conquest of California, Lippincott began to look for some good real estate buys. For awhile his investments were marginal, but then in 1849, he got himself elected to the State's Constitutional Convention in Monterey. That's when he found the real bargains.

As one of 48 delegates, Lippincott sat along side such California luminaries as Mariano Vallejo and John Sutter. He didn't say much, but he listened a lot, especially when the talk turned to removing the capital from Monterey.

When it looked like California's first legislature would meet in San Jose, Lippincott made a beeline for that little hamlet and bought up nearly everything in sight. He invested all he had in the purchase of 31 lots, one of which cost him the outrageous sum of 400 dollars! Then he went back to Monterey in time to sign his name to the document that made California the 31st state in the Union.

Sure enough, after such issues as slavery, state boundaries, voting rights, etc., were dispensed with, the convention took up the matter of moving the capital from Monterey to San Jose. The vote was almost unanimous in favor of the change.

When that first legislature met in San Jose, who but Benjamin S. Lippincott sat as one of the first members of the State Senate? Although he took his job seriously, he did more than just legislate. You see, he put his San Jose property on the market and made a fortune. In a prosperous twist in time, the lot that cost him $400 brought him $2,000. Almost overnight Lippincott became one of the wealthiest men in California, and not one dollar came from the gold fields. Apparently in those early days nobody cared about things like "insider information." One simply had to be in the right place at the right time.

THE PREACHER WHO SOUGHT HIS DUE

California Gold Miners

    The Rev. Colton had been in Monterey for almost two years when he began to hear those stories of gold. One traveler was supposed to have ridden in with $2000 worth. Shortly thereafter, rumor had it that another rough, impoverished-looking fellow showed up with $15,000, and he was alleged to have been followed by a 14 year-old boy who in 54 days had panned out $3,476 in nuggets.

    That did it. Walter Colton decided to go to the gold fields himself. He might just as well, everyone else had gone-- he was having to bake his own bread, grind his own coffee, fry his own bacon, and polish his own boots. All his servants had succumbed to the gold fever long ago.

    On the way, Colton and his entourage had second thoughts, however. They met a weary group of men returning from the mountains who looked like they ought to be knocking at the gates of a pauper's asylum. Most of them had rags bound around their blistered feet and held clubs, with which they beat their skeleton animals, forcing them onward.

When the strangers begged for bread, Colton was sure that he had been taken in by the stories of quick-gotten gain. He was just about to turn around and go back home, but then one of the starving men changed his mind. You see, he poured out a pound or two of nuggets in payment for the bread. These starving men were returning from the diggings with over $100,000 in gold! They were simply on their way to San Francisco to buy supplies, since they couldn't digest precious metals.

Once Colton saw them on their way, in a predictable twist in time, he proceeded once again to the gold fields, this time spurring his horse with urgency. Gone were the doubts-- no more was he an unbeliever. There WAS gold in them thar hills and even a preacher was entitled to his fair share.

CHINESE HURDLE THE SIERRA NEVADA

America's first transcontinental railroad was the result of a race between the Central Pacific and the Union Pacific Railroads. Each company received government subsidies for every mile of track it laid, and they employed hundreds of workers to get the job done.

The Union Pacific, beginning in Omaha, Nebraska, and working west, relied primarily on Irish laborers to lay its tracks. On the other hand, Leland Stanford of the eastward moving Central Pacific knew of a much better source of labor. His only problem was that he had to fight to convince his Superintendent, James Strobridge, to buy his idea.

Stanford knew there were several thousand Chinese in California. Aside from working over the gold gravel pits that no one else would touch, they had been allowed to work only as laundry men, houseboys, and truck gardeners.

Stanford knew them well from his gold mining days. They would be out in the pits at dawn while the white men were still sleeping, and they were still at work at nightfall when the Whites had long since quit.

When Strobridge heard that he might be saddled with pigtailed Chinese who weighed not much over a hundred pounds with which they would be expected to conquer the granite wall of the Sierra Nevada, he exploded in front of his boss with a combination of contempt and rage!

Stanford throttled Strobridge's anger by insisting that the Superintendent give him just 24 hours to make a convincing case for the Chinese workers. Strobridge held his tongue, and Stanford hired fifty Chinese workers, jammed them onto flatcars and took them to the railhead. Dumped out in the midst of a primeval forest, the fatalistic Chinese did not even bother to look at their strange, fearsome surroundings. Instead, they pitched camp, cooked a light supper of dried fish and rice, calmly went to sleep and at dawn were wielding the heavy picks, shovels, and wheelbarrows.

Strobridge stood around looking at these little fellows in their basket hats, pigtails, blue blouses, pantaloons, and soft slippers. He listened to their high birdlike talk and waited for them to collapse from exhaustion. All the while, Stanford had a knowing smile on his face.

At sundown, twelve hours later, after a brutal day's labor that might have floored the huskiest of white men, the Chinese were still going at a good clip.

That night Strobridge went to Stanford and admitted that he had never seen such a demonstration of intensive labor in his life. He was convinced now that the Chinese could do the job, but he still had one question.

"How did you know that these rice-eating weaklings were going to be able to work like this?"

Stanford eyed his loyal subordinate with a twinkle in his eye and responded, "Any race of people who built the Great Wall of China can certainly build a railroad over these mountains."

And in an amazing twist in time, that's exactly what they did.

HELL HATH NO FURY...

A Woman and her Wagon Train

One of the strangest tales in American history is recorded in the diary of Elizabeth Geer. She and her husband and their seven children set out in a covered wagon from Indiana, headed for California in 1847. The wagon train with which the Geers were traveling reached the halfway point by September 15. On the morning of the 16th, one of the men reported that he was having trouble.

His wife was angry at him for trying to drag her half way across the continent and refused to take another step west. Not only would she not budge, she wouldn't allow her children to go either. Her husband had had his oxen hitched up to the wagons for three hours and had been coaxing her to hop aboard, but she wouldn't stir.

Elizabeth told her husband what was taking place, and he gathered three male companions and went to consult with the recalcitrant woman. When she steadfastly refused their entreaties to join them, they grabbed her young ones and crammed them in the wagon. Her husband then drove off and left her sitting.

As the wagons rolled west, the abandoned woman got up, took the back track and traveled out of sight. Meanwhile, the husband sent his oldest son back to where they had camped to retrieve a horse that he had left. In less than an hour, having cut across a bend in the road, the wife overtook her husband. When he saw her he asked, "Did you meet Son John?"

"Yes" was the reply, "and I picked up a stone and knocked out his brains."

Her stunned husband went back to ascertain the truth and got the surprise of his life. You see, while he was gone, his wife set his wagon, which was loaded with all of their store bought goods, on fire. The cover was completely burned, as were some valuable articles. When the man saw the flames, he came running back to put them out. According to Elizabeth, when this was accomplished, "The husband finally mustered spunk enough to do what he should have done in the first place." In a painful twist in time, "he gave his wife what she needed: a good flogging."

Unfortunately, Mrs. Geer doesn't tell us what effect the whipping had on the woman, but one has to wonder if it did any good. After all, anyone who would set fire to her own wagon probably would not be deterred by a few blows from her husband.

IN MEMORY OF THORNBURGH

Thornburgh's Grave

    Hundreds of graves are strung out all along the Oregon Trail. Death was no respecter of persons. Men, women, and children alike met untimely deaths and were laid to rest along the road. Some of their stones still mark the graves, and they are all sad monuments to the brave pioneer spirit, especially Old Thornburgh's.

    When he wasn't running with his mountain men buddies in the Rockies, Old Thornburgh lived at Fort Bridger in what is now southwestern Wyoming. Although he wasn't in the army, all of the soldiers stationed at the fort respected and valued his friendship. Someone as impervious to danger as he was could always be counted on, and that's why the troopers took a liking to him.

    Thornburgh first showed his mettle when he joined a company of soldiers that had been sent out to escort a wagon train through hostile Indian territory nearby. As the pioneers made their way along the trail and no trouble was encountered, all of the troopers, with one exception, turned around and headed back to the fort. The soldier who remained was the company commander, but he wasn't left by himself. Old Thornburgh stayed right by his side, just in case.

    After another hour or two passed without an Indian attack, the Major motioned for Thornburgh to follow him. Leaving the wagon train in safety, the two headed back towards the fort. Then tragedy struck. The Indians were there all the time, but the presence of a large contingent of soldiers had prevented them from leaving their hiding place. Now when they saw only Thornburgh and the Major, they whistled a different tune.

It was a quick hit and run attack, and Old Thornburgh came through it unscathed. The Major, however, was killed. At that point, Thornburgh was thrust on the horns of a dilemma. If he left the Major's body, the Indians might return and mutilate it. On the other hand, if he remained, it might cost him his life.

Old Thornburgh didn't even think about it. He remained right there by the Major's side until someone from the fort came looking for them. For that act of bravery, Thornburgh won the respect of everyone at Fort Bridger.

That was not the only time that Thornburgh proved his worth. Once he saved a child from drowning in a nearby creek, and on another occasion, when two trappers were engaged in a drunken brawl, he put a stop to the fracas by attacking one of the men who had drawn a knife.

No, there was no doubt about it. Even though he was a civilian, Old Thornburgh was worth his weight in gold.

Then came that fateful day in 1887. Old Thornburgh was ambling across the quadrangle at the fort and got too close to an ornery mule. With one powerful kick, the animal sent Thornburgh flying across the compound and into eternity.

A gloomy pall settled within the palisades of the fort, and in gratitude for Thornburgh's loyalty, the troopers buried him there and marked his grave with a headstone, a footstone, and a white picket fence.

Today, those traveling the Oregon Trial by auto can visit Old Thornburgh's grave. There is no trace of the Major's final resting place, but Thornburgh's has been preserved for posterity, for you see, Thornburgh—the loyal friend to all at Fort Bridger—was not a human. In a surprising twist in time, those who visit his grave will find that he was a faithful Collie, which proves once again that a dog is man's best friend.

ROBES OF RIGHTEOUSNESS FELL IN UTAH

In the summer of 1857, the Fancher Wagon Train of about 140 men, women, and children were making their way west. They had started out in Arkansas, headed for California. When they reached Salt Lake City, they were advised to go north and hit the California Trail. Instead, they turned south and met an untimely end at the hands of an unlikely foe.

Mountain Meadows Massacre

The members of the Fancher Train knew that they were traveling in Mormon territory. They also knew that the Latter Day Saints were having problems with the United States Government over polygamy, which made them suspicious of every "Gentile" wagon train traversing their land.

What the immigrants didn't know was the further south they traveled from Salt Lake City, the further away they moved from the protective hand of Brigham Young. South of the capital there were Mormon enclaves such as Cedar City and Harmony in which there lived scores of "Saints" who had had their fill of religious and political enemies. By the summer of 1857, as the Fancher Party approached their settlements, these southern Mormons decided to strike back.

Sensing that serious trouble was brewing, Isaac Haight, the Mormon leader in Cedar City, sent word to Brigham Young, asking for instructions as to how to deal with the "invaders." In the meantime, one "Major" John D. Lee stepped forth to seize the day.

Lee made a pact with the local Indians to annihilate the immigrants. First, the Native Americans attacked the wagon train off and on for three days in a meadow about 30 miles from Cedar City.

According to plan, Lee suddenly appeared waving a flag of truce. During his parley with the Fanchers, Lee promised relief. All they had to do was follow his instructions.

Following the lead of the evil genius, the Fancher party turned over its weapons and lined up outside the circle of wagons. Beside each immigrant was an armed Mormon. Side by side, the "Gentiles" and the "Saints" were to march to safety, but suddenly there came a cry. "Do your duty," shouted Lee, and the Mormon "protectors" turned on the immigrants, killing every man, woman, and child in the party.

Two days after the massacre, a message from Brigham Young arrived ordering the Mormons of Cedar City to leave the Fancher party unmolested. That's when Lee went to Salt Lake City to explain. He laid it all on the Indians and denied any complicity, but it didn't work, although it took twenty years for justice to be done.

After two trials and two decades, John D. Lee was convicted of the mass murder, and on March 23, 1877, he was executed at Mountain Meadows on the very spot where he had led the massacre of the Fancher Party.

When Brigham Young died in the year of Lee's execution, it added a touch of irony to the story. You see, he had always condemned the Mountain Meadows Massacre and saw to it that Lee was excommunicated from the church before his execution. However in an unfortunate twist in time, the Mormon leader was never able to erase the stain Lee placed on the church. Once the robes of righteousness fell, it was difficult to gather them up.

THE PRICE OF DISCOVERING YOSEMITE VALLEY

Perhaps the most lasting result of the Indian War of 1851 was the discovery of Yosemite Valley by Europeans, although it most assuredly would have been found sooner or later. Indeed, some say that Joseph Reddeford Walker was the first to lay eyes on it in 1833. Nearly everyone, however, agrees that it was Major James Savage who really made the discovery in 1851, and when he did, he found a lot more than that for which he had bargained.

The date was March 19, 1851, and Jim Savage was fit to be tied. He had issued an order through an Indian courier that Teneya, Chief of the Yosemites, bring his entire tribe into camp and make a treaty to end officially the war between the Mariposa Battalion and his tribe. The Chief obeyed the summons himself, but he brought none of his tribesmen with him. An annoyed Major Savage gave Teneya three days to fully comply with his order or suffer a resumption of hostilities.

Yosemite Valley

Savage had no sooner allowed Teneya to go back for his people than he had second thoughts, so he set out to follow the Indian leader. After a few days he met Teneya dutifully leading his tribe to a rendezvous with Savage, but the Major remained suspicious. He doubted that all of the Indians had left their rancheria, so he grabbed Teneya and turned him around.

After a three-day march, Savage's detail, guided by Chief Teneya, entered the Yosemite Valley. It was recorded as "Being of surpassing beauty, about 10 miles in length and one mile broad." Upon either side were high perpendicular rocks and at each end through which the Middle Fork of the Merced River ran, were deep canyons. It was a stunning sight—almost as stunning as what Savage found in a near-by cave.

He had been right. Not all of the Indians had left their home. There in the dead of winter, amidst the beauty of Yosemite, sat an old Indian couple—the parents of Chief Teneya. They alone had remained—to die. You see, "Teneya had thrown them away since they could not travel and take care of themselves."

They had a small fire burning, but it was having little effect. Savage had a large pile of wood and some acorns carried to them, but they were too advanced in age. In a tragic twist in time, his order that the Yosemite Indians abandon their ancestral homelands had been a death sentence for the elderly duo, and all the wood and acorns in the world could not change that now.

CHARACTER BUILDING ON THE FRONTIER

Solomon Young's Grave

Solomon Young was a 19th century pioneer who earned his living with his freight wagon. He started out on the Santa Fe Trail, hauling goods to New Mexico and even made one trip to California. In all of these ventures, Solomon enjoyed only a modicum of success, but he still had his pride. He never let it be said that he wasn't a man of his word, and the firmness of that conviction found its way to the White House a hundred years later.

After years of toil on the trail, in 1860 opportunity pounded fervently at Solomon's door. Unrest had erupted in Utah between the United States government and the Mormons. Troops had been sent in to establish control of the desert that Brigham Young and his followers had made to blossom. Solomon eyed these developments and decided to seize the day. There was a fortune to be made by hauling supplies to the army in Utah.

Solomon's first move was to enlist investors in his project. He needed forty wagons and $30,000 worth of goods and salt pork. This was no easy task, but Solomon gained the necessary backing by personally guaranteeing the success of the venture. People trusted him to do what he promised.

That spring Solomon headed for Salt Lake City with his wagon train loaded down with supplies, but alas there was trouble in paradise. For some reason, the army officer in charge refused to accept the provisions that Solomon had hauled from Independence. Suddenly the freight man realized that he was on the horns of a dilemma. Here he was, hundreds of miles from home, deeply in debt, and responsible for the disposition of the cargo he had carried across the plains.

His bright idea now teetered on the verge of disaster, and he had to find some solution. Clearly the buck stopped with Solomon Young. He couldn't bear the thought of going home in defeat. People back in Independence were counting on him. That's why he went to see Brigham Young.

When apprised of Solomon's dilemma, Brigham agreed to take the whole shipment. The Mormon leader could have only respect for a man who was willing to take responsibility for his actions. Besides that, he needed the supplies.

Solomon Young returned to Independence where he lived out his life. Long after he was gone, the story of his brush with financial ruin in Utah became the basis for a family tradition. His daughter, Martha Ellen, never let it be forgotten that her father, Solomon, always met his responsibilities. His Utah experience became an object lesson in character building for his descendants, for you see, Solomon Young was the grandfather of Harry S. Truman.

In an unpredictable twist in time, the old pioneer's determination to meet his obligations became a family legend, and by the 20th century it evolved into a sign on the President's desk, which said, "The buck stops here."

CUSTER AND THE ROOSTER

George Armstrong Custer—his name has been indelibly engraved on the pages of American history. Brave, dashing, and often foolhardy, he is best remembered for leading several companies of the Seventh U.S. Cavalry to complete annihilation in the Battle of the Little Big Horn. That tragedy, however, probably would never have occurred if only the authorities at West Point had caught Custer with that rooster.

After Custer was appointed to West Point in 1857, he was constantly on the brink of dismissal because of excessive demerits. In 1861, his last year at the Point, things looked bleak. One more demerit and he would have been sent packing. Custer was on edge, and that's one reason Henry Douglass' rooster got on his nerves and provoked him so easily.

Cadet Custer lived in the 8th Division barracks facing the quarters of Lt. Henry Douglass. Now it just so happened that Douglass kept a rooster whose raucous crowing caused Custer to lose sleep. One night he decided that he had had enough. He crept up to Douglass' window and grabbed his bird, took it back to his own room and cooked it over a gas burner.

With the offensive bird out of the way, Custer collected the feathers, rolled them up in a newspaper and convinced one of the other cadets to take the evidence out to a trash bin for disposal. Hurrying across the open field to avoid detection, Custer's buddy strung a trail of feathers behind him.

Fortunately, or unfortunately, for Custer he was never caught and punished because the feathered trail led to his fellow cadet. He went ahead and graduated at the bottom of his class. Had Custer's act been discovered, he would have been given sufficient demerits to have pushed him over the limit for that period. This would have led to Custer's expulsion and the end of his military career.

Custer's Funeral Cortege at West Point

So you see, Custer was never blamed for the rooster caper. As a result, he gained quite a reputation fighting Rebels during the Civil War and later the Plains Indians. This latter episode, of course, cost him and over 200 other troopers their lives.

Thus in a fatal twist in time, the silencing of that rooster in 1861, and the cadet code of secrecy saved Custer for a much worse fate than expulsion from West Point. It seems a pity that the rooster didn't crow a little louder on the night of its demise.

MOSES SCHALLENBERGER'S MOUNTAIN MONUMENT

Moses Schallenberger was born in 1826. At the age of 15, he was orphaned and went to live with his sister, Louise and her husband, Dr. John Townsend. That's how he came to be on the road to California in 1844, and that's how he got snowbound in the Sierra Nevada—two years before the Donner party disaster.

Schallenberger's brother-in -law, John Townsend, talked the family into joining the Stevens-Murphy party to California in 1844. He wanted to move west for commercial purposes. Most of their trip was as uneventful as overland journeys ever got, until they hit the Sierra Nevada. There Townsend found it impossible to breach the mountains with his wagons, loaded as they were with merchandise for sale in California, so he decided to leave them at what is now Donner Lake. He also decided to leave Moses and two of his buddies, Joseph Foster and Allen Montgomery, to watch over his property until he could return to claim it.

Moses Schallenberger At Truckey's Lake, 1844-45

The three teenagers had no sooner erected a crude cabin than a huge blizzard dropped three feet of snow on them. Concerned that they might be caught in the wilderness with no food, they decided to build some snowshoes out of wagon bows and hike to Sutter's Fort. Foster and Montgomery made it, but Moses had to turn back the first day due to illness. While his buddies went on, he limped back to the cabin to spend his 18th birthday alone at the summit of the treacherous Sierra Nevada Mountains.

WWW.TWISTINTIME.COM

Schallenberger stayed alive by trapping foxes and an occasional coyote. Finally, in the spring of 1845, Dennis Martin, another member of his company, came back for him and guided him to Sutter's Fort. As for the valued merchandise that he was charged with protecting, it had disappeared; the Indians saw to that.

The cabin, however, was left unmolested. You see, it stood there, not only as a monument to the courage of young Moses Schallenberger, the first California bound pioneer to be stuck in the mountains, but in a strange twist in time, it served as a much needed refuge the next year for another snowbound group—the Donner Party.

BUFFALO BILL'S ELUSIVE HONOR

Buffalo Bill

William Frederick Cody, better known as "Buffalo Bill," was a legendary character straight out of the Old West. He rode for the Pony Express, fought Indians, hunted buffalo, scouted for the Army, and thanks to dime novelist, Ned Buntline, became one of the nation's foremost folk heroes. By the time of his death in 1917, Cody's name had become a household word, but then the U.S. Government chose to cast a shadow across his image by taking back his Congressional Medal of Honor.

Buffalo Bill was born in Iowa in 1846. When his father died in 1857, he moved with his mother to Kansas. Three years later he began his dramatic rise to fame by joining the Pony Express. When the telegraph put that operation out of business, Bill returned home where he became one of the most efficient buffalo hunters on the plains. Then came the Civil War.

Cody enlisted in the Seventh Kansas Cavalry and saw considerable action in Missouri and Tennessee. After the war, he continued to work for the Army as a scout and dispatch carrier, operating out of Fort Ellsworth, Kansas. Finally, in 1867, Bill took up the trade that would give him his nickname—hunting buffalo to feed the construction crews of the Kansas Pacific Railroad. By his own count, he killed 4,280 of the animals in 17 months.

Then in 1868, Cody returned to work for the Army and secured his place in the annals of American military history by leading the U.S. Fifth Cavalry in pursuit of Tall Bull, Chief of the Cheyenne Dog Soldiers. Through Cody's prowess on the trail, the soldiers cornered the Cheyenne at Summit Springs, Colorado, and defeated them. The United States Government recognized William Frederick Cody's service to the Army by awarding him the Congressional Medal of Honor for gallantry.

With more than 15 years of highly publicized western adventures under his belt, Cody went into show business. From 1875 to 1882, he traveled the country with his "Wild West, Rocky Mountain, and Prairie Exhibition." Between 1883 and 1913, his tours included not only the United States, but Europe as well.

When Buffalo Bill Cody died on January 10, 1917, in Denver, the Colorado legislature passed a special resolution authorizing his body to lie in state in the capitol building for one day. During that time, 25,000 people passed by his casket to pay their respects. It seemed a fitting tribute to the man whose exploits had thrilled the nation. Then the United States Government plucked that feather from his war bonnet.

You see, within a few months after his death, authorities in Washington, D.C. revoked the Congressional Medal of Honor that had been one of William F. Cody's most prized possessions for over 40 years. Citing the fact that he had been a civilian and not a military scout when he won the medal, Cody's name was stricken from the roll of Medal of Honor recipients, and it remained that way for 72 years.

Then in a bizarre twist in time, President George Herbert Walker Bush, sensing that an injustice had been committed, restored Cody's medal, and today it can be seen at the Buffalo Bill Historical Center in Cody, Wyoming. Perhaps the White House didn't relish the thought of the United States Government carrying the opprobrium of being an "Indian giver."

SIDESTEPPING TRAGEDY ON A MISSISSIPPI RIVERBOAT

19th Century Mississippi Riverboat

The Mississippi River had a strange attraction for any number of young American boys in the 19th century. Many of them were drawn to the river boats that plied those mighty waters. That's what happened to Sam and his younger brother, Henry, in 1858. They landed jobs on the *Pennsylvania*, a side wheel packet, and thought they had the world by the tail, until Sam got fired.

Dejected and disappointed, Sam signed on with another boat. Eight days later, however, he was thanking his lucky stars that he had been put ashore, for one of the boilers on the *Pennsylvania* exploded killing dozens of people. Thus, while his brother Henry became one of the casualties, Sam lived to make his way onto the pages of American history.

It was four o'clock in the morning on Sunday, June 13, 1858, when that boiler exploded. Henry was asleep down below. Somehow he got into the water and made it to shore. He and thirty-two other scalded men were taken to Memphis and placed side by side in a single room.

Two days later, who should show up but Sam? He had been on another steamer, the *A.T. Lacey*, and was just a little more than a day behind the *Pennsylvania* when its boiler blew. At Memphis he got off his boat and went to find Henry. He located him stretched out on a blanket on the floor with the other wounded men, all of whom were attended by a Dr. Peyton with his staff of younger physicians.

Sam stayed by Henry's side for five days, but there was nothing that could be done. In an attempt to relieve his pain, one of the doctors gave him a heavy dose of morphine one night. He was dead before dawn.

Sam helped carry Henry to the "dead room," and then he went home with one of the locals to sleep off his accumulated fatigue. The next day he took Henry to St. Louis where he purchased a coffin and then transported him to their home in Hannibal, Missouri, where he dressed Henry in one of his own suits and buried him beside their father, John M. Clemens.

After that Sam Clemens returned to the river boats but not for long. In a short time he was in California writing stories under a pen name.

You see, as Mark Twain, Sam went on to catch the attention of the literary world with his stories of Huckleberry Finn, Becky Thatcher, and Tom Sawyer. In a nostalgic twist in time, however, he never forgot his days on the Mississippi River, especially that time when a quarrel with the pilot of the *Pennsylvania* separated him from his younger brother, allowing him to fulfill his destiny.

RANK HAD ITS PRIVILEGES

The Brooklyn

During the westward migrations of the 1840s, travelers came by land and by sea. Those coming overland knew what an ordeal they were in for, but the hardships of the sea voyage weren't generally known until one began the trip. As it turned out, privations at sea were every bit as wearing on the human spirit as anything that happened on the trail, unless, of course one happened to be in charge.

It was a very irritated company of 220 Latter-day Saints who passed through the Golden Gate on July 24, 1846. Their voyage to California had been every bit as demanding as anything experienced by any member of a wagon train, but what really had them steamed was their leader, Elder Sam Brannan.

They had left with him from New York on February 4, and it didn't take them long to find out that the conditions on the ship were in a terrible state. One passenger wrote, "The drinking water was thick and ropy with slime, so that it had to be strained between the teeth, and the taste was dreadful...Rats abounded in the vessel; cockroaches and smaller vermin infested the provisions, until eternal vigilance was the price imposed upon every mouthful."

This was accompanied by miserable quarters below the deck. "So low were the ceilings," wrote another diarist, "that only a dwarf could stand erect, and a person of normal stature must move about by crouching monkey-fashion." It was always semi-dark below and could only be dimly lit by the whale oil lamps. After meals and prayers the families could only go to the tiny bunks with canvas curtains. It was all poorly ventilated and highly unsanitary.

All of that would have been all right, however, if only their leader had shared their misery. You see, at the beginning of the voyage Elder Samuel Brannan ate and slept with the rest of the passengers. But when the conditions became unbearable, Brannan was soon dining at the captain's table and sleeping in his cabin in relative comfort most of the time.

And there he remained throughout the remainder of the voyage, safe, secure, and comfortable while his fellow travelers suffered and grumbled under unspeakable conditions.

In a perplexing twist in time, no one had told them that rank did have its privileges, even among the Saints who believed that God was no respecter of person.

SHAKING HANDS
AT THE WRONG TIME

Julius Caesar Burrows was a well-known politician in the 19th century. He was raised in Pennsylvania and as an adult, practiced law in Michigan. When the Civil War broke out, he served as a Union infantry captain, and after Appomattox, he was elected to the United States House of Representatives where he made his reputation as a brilliant orator. So effective was his public speaking that in 1876, New Mexico was denied statehood all because one poor fellow came in on the tail end of one of his speeches.

New Mexico had been trying for 26 years to move from territorial status to statehood. In 1850, it failed in its first attempt, and subsequent efforts were just as disappointing. Then in 1876, the picture looked good. It appeared that New Mexico stood an excellent chance of becoming a state, and that might have been the case if only Stephen B. Elkins had been around to listen to all of Congressman Burrows' speech.

At issue was a bill intended to protect the civil rights of freed black slaves. Southerners were, of course, vociferous in their opposition to the proposal, while representatives from the North were just as adamant in their support. Although the debate was hot and heavy, Elkins, who represented New Mexico as a territorial delegate, missed most of it. While Burrows was speaking, he was busy outside the chambers trying to line up votes for the New Mexico Statehood Bill.

Meanwhile Burrows was bringing proponents of the legislation to a fever pitch with his oratorical skills. As he reached the climax of his speech, the roar of approval was deafening. Elkins, hearing the pandemonium that had broken loose, hurried to the chamber. Unaware of the full import of the speech, Elkins grabbed Burrows and began pumping his hand in ignorance. This, of course, was the kiss of death for the statehood measure.

As Elkins returned to his seat, he met the cold stares of the Southern congressmen who were already calculating as to how they might exact their revenge on this upstart who obviously was lavish in his support of Burrows' waving of the "bloody shirt."

After Congress disposed of the civil rights bill, it turned to two statehood proposals—one from New Mexico and one from Colorado. In the case of the latter, it passed easily, but the southern delegation turned thumbs down on a similar bill for New Mexico. You see, that hardy handshake that Elkins gave Burrows was enough to drive a stake through the heart of the New Mexico statehood bill. In a strange twist in time, while Colorado achieved statehood in 1876, New Mexico remained a territory for another 36 years, due in no small measure to an ill-timed and misinterpreted handshake.

Julius Caesar Burrows

WILLIAM TODD'S PIG

California Bear Flag Revolt

On the night of June 14, 1846, General Mariano Vallejo was rudely awakened by a banging on the front door of his Sonoma home. As he peered out, he saw a group of "Bear Flaggers," who were intent on turning California into a Republic. They were armed to the teeth and ready to do business. In fact, the only thing they lacked was an artist to make their flag.

Vallejo opened the door and was informed that he was under arrest, so he sat down at his table to compose a treaty of capitulation.

When he was through, he handed the document over to the leader, William Ide, and then was taken to Sutter's Fort where he was incarcerated. The Bear Flag Revolt had begun, but something was radically wrong! The new nation had no flag, so the insurgents proceeded to fill the void.

A Mrs. Elliott was prevailed upon to cut a piece of white cloth from a bolt of cotton she had in her home. A red stripe for the bottom was provided by Mrs. Josefa Mathews, while paint was secured from another home.

The Americans wanted a star to go on their flag such as the Texans had produced on their banner; this was put in the upper left-hand corner. Then an obscure American with a famous name took his place on the stage of history. He tried to draw a Grizzly bear to the right of the star, but alas, his artistic skill left something to be desired. When he was finished, the Grizzly bear looked for all the world, exactly like a pig!

The short-lived Bear Flag revolt retired its emblem when the United States officially usurped its prerogative of conquest, but when California joined the Union, it was hauled out of moth balls and became the model for the state's official flag.

This time, however, someone besides William Todd drew the bear. For you see, he had been the one who illustrated the California Bear Flag, and even though he was the nephew of Mrs. Abraham Lincoln, he had no artistic talent, and in that aesthetic twist in time, nobody wanted the likeness of a hog as the symbol of our 31st state.

Modern Oddities
With A Twist

HOCKEY'S BLOODY ST. PATRICK'S DAY

Clarence Campbell

Clarence Campbell was really looking forward to attending the 1955, St. Patrick's Day hockey game in Montreal between the Canadians and the Detroit Red Wings. The two teams were locked in a bitter struggle for the National Hockey League's top spot, and Campbell arrived expecting an exciting time. After he took his seat in the arena, however, it didn't take him long to wish that he had never come.

When Clarence showed up, the game had already begun, and Detroit was leading 2-1. The fans were not at all happy, and when near the end of the first period the Red Wings increased their lead to 4-1, the crowd grew ugly. That's when they spotted Campbell.

Simultaneously, the fans began to yell his name. "We want Campbell; we want Campbell." Soon some of them moved toward him, and one fellow reached out as if to shake his hand. When Clarence responded, the man, instead of shaking hands, landed a blow to Campbell's jaw. Then the fracas began in earnest. The fans began to take their frustration out on Clarence.

In a moment, Campbell was surrounded by the wild-eyed hockey crowd, and they were blaming him for their team's poor St. Patrick's Day showing. The next moment bunches of tomatoes, eggs, bottles of water, and of all things, pickled pigs feet were being hurled his way. Others began to take swings at him. Things were beginning to look desperate for this man who simply wanted to watch a hockey game.

The attack on Clarence Campbell could have ended up costing him his life. He was being mobbed, and the police couldn't help him, until one of them let loose with some tear gas. With that everyone left the arena, including Clarence, who was escorted to his home in a shaken but otherwise unhurt condition.

The crowd, once in the street, turned its hostility on anything that moved and some things that didn't. They damaged cars, burned newsstands, wrecked phone booths and looted stores. They were determined to make someone pay for what Clarence Campbell had done to their hockey team. After all, it was his fault that Maurice Richard, their star player had been suspended for the rest of the season.

In an earlier game, during one of those interminable hockey scuffles that break out from time to time, Richard had struck an official, and that's when Clarence Campbell stepped in. As President of the National Hockey League, it was his job to discipline Richard, thus the suspension for the remainder of the season.

The hostility that subsequently erupted in Montreal on Thursday, March 17, 1955, has been called "Hockey's Bloody St. Patrick's Day." It did nothing, however to assuage the anger of the fans of that city, nor did it change Clarence Campbell's mind. He defied public opinion and held fast to his ruling. Richard didn't return to the ice that season, and to add insult to injury, Detroit won the Stanley Cup.

GENERAL PATTON LOST THE RACE

General George S. Patton is one of the most enigmatic figures in the history of the United States military. He was deeply religious yet egregiously profane. He had a genuine love for his men yet drove them at times beyond endurance. Most of the time, Patton appeared to be ego maniacal, but when the chips were down, the General could swallow his pride and exhibit magnanimous gestures of acceptance. An excellent example of this occurred when a long time friend who had been his junior officer for years passed him up for promotion during World War II and became his boss.

George S. Patton

Patton and his friend met in 1919 in Washington D.C. They took to each other instantly, although Patton was six years his friend's senior in the Army. The junior officer looked up to Patton and recognized that he was the leading mind in tank warfare.

Between 1935 and 1940 the two men became extremely close. Although he was the senior officer, Patton and his friend spent summer vacations together with their families. In 1938, Patton was promoted to full Colonel, and his friend moved up to Lieutenant Colonel. The junior officer openly admitted that he saw Patton as a friend, superior officer, and mentor.

With World War II on the horizon, the Army recognized Patton's genius for tank warfare, and they quickly made him a Brigadier General. In less than a year, he put on the two stars of a Major General. In 1940, the friend, who was still a Lieutenant Colonel petitioned Major General Patton for the opportunity to serve under the tank corps commander. Patton readily accepted, stating that he would like nothing better than for his friend to be placed under his command, but then fate stepped in; General George Marshall had other ideas for Patton's friend.

In 1941, after five years as a relatively unknown Lieutenant Colonel, Patton's friend was promoted to Colonel and six months later appointed as a Brigadier General and assigned to the General Staff in Washington D.C. Patton was still senior to his friend, but this was soon to change. In 1942, the friend received a promotion to Major General and, then a few months later, he was promoted past Patton to Lieutenant General.

When the Allies announced the invasion of North Africa, Major General Patton suddenly found himself under the command of his former subordinate, now one star his senior. In a year and a half, Patton's friend had moved from obscurity as a Lieutenant Colonel to a Lieutenant General in command of the Allied Forces in North Africa.

The next year Patton almost caught his friend. He was promoted to Lieutenant General, but one month before, his friend had been promoted to four-star General.

The rest of Patton's story is well known. He was accused of slapping a soldier in Sicily, and his friend, who was now his immediate superior, relieved him of command of the Seventh Army. Later the friend gave Patton another chance and made him commander of the Third Army. With the end of the war, however, their long friendship finally came to an end. Patton made some injudicious political remarks, and his friend fired him.

Within a few months, Patton was dead, having succumbed to injuries suffered in a jeep accident. His friend, on the other hand, went on to become General of the Army and later President of the United States. For you see, Patton's friend, who was for such a long time his subordinate, was none other than Dwight David Eisenhower. In an astounding twist in time, Ike had leaped to the top. As for Patton, perhaps the bard was right; "There is a Divinity that shapes our ends, rough hew them as we will."

AMERICA'S ANNUAL HALLOWEEN SÉANCE

Witches! Goblins! Ghosts! They are all part of a Halloween tradition that has grown up over the years. At sunset each October 31st, children put on costumes and go "trick or treating." For the most part, it is a night of innocent make-believe, unless one is part of those annual séances that are held each Halloween in various cities across the nation. Folks who attend these gatherings take the night very seriously. Since 1927, they have been trying to make contact on the last day of every October with their deceased hero, Ehrich Weiss.

Weiss was born on March 24, 1874, in Budapest, Hungary. His family immigrated to the United States when he was four years old and settled in Appleton, Wisconsin, where his father served as rabbi of the Jewish Reform Congregation. In 1887, the Weiss family moved to New York City, and in 1893, Ehrich met Bess Rahner. He married her three weeks later.

Ehrich became a stage performer of considerable renown, but his real love was for the two women in his life—his wife and his mother. When the latter died in 1920, Ehrich was thrown into a state of depression, and in desperation he and Bess contacted several spiritualists in an attempt to reach his mother across the Great Divide. When none of the mediums were able to provide the couple with a message from the dead, his faith in spiritualism turned to cynicism. Ehrich shifted his energies toward debunking self-proclaimed psychics and mediums. As a result, in addition to his stage fame, he gained a national reputation as a "ghost buster."

Then on Halloween, 1926, at the age of 52, Ehrich Weiss died of peritonitis from a ruptured appendix. That set the stage for one final sting for his spiritualist opponents. Shortly before his death, he made a pact with Bess that he would contact her from the other side if possible and deliver a pre-arranged coded message. For the next ten years, Bess held a séance on Halloween to test the pact.

Finally in 1936, after a final unsuccessful attempt to

contact her husband from the roof of the Knickerbocker Hotel in Hollywood, Bess extinguished the candle that she had kept burning beside a photograph of her husband since his death. Later she explained that "ten years is long enough to wait for any man."

Such was not the case, however, for the thousands of diehard followers of Ehrich Weiss, for you see, to this day they continue to hold annual séances each October 31st, in hopes that the great illusionist will pull one more trick out of the proverbial hat.

So far, this has not happened, and one suspects that it won't. Although in an amazing twist in time the man whose stage name was Harry Houdini got himself out of any number of tight spots while he was among the living, one suspects that it will take more than some fanciful twisting and turning to escape the chains of death—even on Halloween night.

Harry Houdini

THE PRESIDENT'S DAUGHTER HAD THE LAST WORD

Alice Roosevelt

In September 1901, news of the nation's tragedy swept across America. President William McKinley had died from a gunshot wound inflicted on him earlier by a deranged anarchist. For eight days the people watched as the Grim Reaper beckoned the President to the eternal regions.

Nobody was more anxious for McKinley's recovery than the Vice President, and no one was *happier* on the occasion of his death that the Vice President's daughter, Alice Lee Roosevelt, much to TR's chagrin.

Alice Roosevelt had always been a handful, in part because of the tragedy that accompanied her arrival on February 12, 1884. Two days later both her mother and her grandmother died in the same house on the same day. Her heartbroken father gave Alice to his sister for her to raise and went west for two years to camp and hunt. When he returned, he married Edith Crow and resumed his role as a husband and father.

At Edith's insistence, all allusions to the first Mrs. Roosevelt ceased. After a time, it was as if she never existed. Alice never quite got over this annihilation of her own identity, for she had been named after her mother but was never called Alice in her father's house again. Instead, folks referred to her as "Sister" or "Baby Lee."

Alice Lee never forgave her father for his painful abandonment of her and for allowing Edith to attack the memory of her mother so blatantly. She made no secret that she, in fact, had no use for her father. She told her friends that Theodore Roosevelt was "impossible to be around." She referred to him as "radioactive," "TNT," and "a steam engine in pants."

When TR was sworn in as Vice President, daughter Alice was heard to say, "Now he will want to be the baby at every christening, the bride at every wedding, and the corpse at every funeral."

No, there was no doubt about it. Roosevelt definitely had a public relations problem with his own daughter, and she proved it when he ascended to the Presidency.

You see, when William McKinley died, reporters besieged the Roosevelt home for an appropriate expression of grief from the new President. After TR expressed his sorrow, the newsmen found the teenaged Alice on the front lawn. The reporters inquired sadly of her, "And how does young Miss Roosevelt feel about this terrible tragedy that afflicts the nation?"

In an iconoclastic twist in time, Alice looked up and replied, "Utter rapture! Daddy always wanted to be President, and now he is."

Alice Lee Roosevelt may not have been a politician, but she knew precisely what she was doing. She wasn't about to pass up an opportunity to go for the jugular vein when the opportunity presented itself.

THE REAL LEGACY OF PEARL HARBOR

Japanese Zero

December 7, 1941, "A day that will live in infamy!" That's what President Franklin Delano Roosevelt called it.

As most everyone knows, on that day Japan struck the blow that brought the United States into World War II, but the Land of the Rising Sun was not through with America yet. Within six months, the U.S. suffered another sneak attack on its territory and a subsequent humiliation, the likes of which had not been endured since the War of 1812.

Six months after inflicting heavy damage on America's Pacific fleet, Japan, flushed with victory, turned its military eye to the north. Since it had already aroused the American population with its surprise raid on Pearl, it decided to go for broke and begin an invasion of the United States. To accomplish this, the Japanese chose to start in the Aleutian Islands and work their way up to Alaska from whence they could then attack the continental United States from land bases. On June 3, 1942, Japanese planes suddenly attacked U.S. Army and Navy installations at Dutch Harbor, located on an island southwest of the Alaskan Peninsula. The Anchorage Daily Times, in a 72 point headline, warned the country, "Japs Raid Dutch Harbor!"

Unexpected heavy resistance prevented the Japanese from following up their air attack with a ground invasion of Dutch Harbor, so they moved further down the Aleutian archipelago to establish bases. On June 6, 1942, Japanese soldiers landed on Kiska and on the next day Attu fell. For the next year, Japan occupied this conquered U.S. territory and prepared to move northeast. Then the Eleventh Air Force moved to stop the invading enemy. By May 1943, America had had enough.

Over 27,000 bombs were dropped on Kiska and Attu in an attempt to soften Japanese emplacements prior to amphibious landings of U.S. forces, which came on May 11, 1943. Eighteen days later, the Americans had retaken Attu. Of the 2,300 Japanese soldiers occupying the island, fewer than 30 survived. The U.S. then turned on Kiska.

With the expulsion of the Japanese from Attu, the Americans increased their bombardment of Kiska. Japanese cruisers and destroyers were forced to evacuate their soldiers, and by July 28, 1943, the last of the Japanese occupation forces had left U.S. territory and were on their way home.

For more than a year, the Japanese had done what no other nation had been able to do since the British occupied Washington D.C. in the War of 1812. In an unthinkable twist in time, they invaded and occupied sovereign U.S. territory. In the end, however, they had to face what Admiral Isoroku Yamamoto called the "sleeping giant," which they had awakened a year earlier at Pearl Harbor, and that "giant" arose to set things right. Such was the real legacy of December 7, 1941.

THE NEW YORK TIMES EATS ITS WORDS

Robert Goddard

Robert Goddard, the "Father of Modern Rocketry," became interested in outer space after reading H.G. Wells' The War of the Worlds. Goddard went on to earn his Ph.D. and began to design rocket motors, hoping some day to set the stage for space travel. Initially he hit a brick wall in his attempt to convince folks that he was on to something, especially the New York Times, who pilliored him in 1919, as a hopeless dreamer whose mental elevator wasn't exactly reaching the top floor.

"Everybody knows rockets won't travel in the vacuum of space, where there's nothing to push against," wrote the Times. Goddard, the paper claimed, "seems to lack the knowledge ladled out daily in high schools." Soon nearly all of the print media hopped on the Times' anti-Goddard bandwagon, but they would one day live to regret it.

Goddard launched the first liquid-fueled rocket on March 16, 1926, at Auburn, Massachusetts. He simply noted in his diary that "The first flight with a rocket using liquid propellants was made yesterday at Aunt Effic's farm." The rocket, which rose just 41 feet, stayed in the air for two and a half seconds and then landed in a cabbage patch.

Goddard continued to press on toward his goal but continued to find little support among the public, who doubted the viability of rocket travel in space. After one of his experiments in 1929, a local Worcester newspaper carried the headline "Moon rocket misses target by 238,799 1/2 miles."

Eventually Goddard relocated to Roswell, New Mexico but was still rejected by his fellow countrymen. Ironically, it was Nazi Germany that took the most interest in his research. Before 1939, German scientists would occasionally even contact Goddard directly with technical questions.

Unfortunately Robert Goddard never lived to reap the rewards of his work. He developed throat cancer in 1945, and died on August 10, the day after the atomic bomb was dropped on Nagasaki. His work, however was carried on by others who eventually publicly recognized their indebtedness to Goddard.

Then in 1969, fifty years after the New York Times had first ridiculed him and his ideas, Goddard got his revenge, posthumously. Just days before the Apollo 11 Moon landing, The New York Times swallowed its pride and retracted its 1919 editorial about Goddard. "Further investigation and experimentation" the paper wrote, "have confirmed the 17th century findings of Sir Isaac Newton, and it is now definitely established that a rocket can function in a vacuum as well as in an atmosphere. The Times regrets the error."

It is too bad that The New York Times wasn't there when Robert Goddard gave his high school graduation oration, which he entitled "On Taking Things for Granted." In a forward looking twist in time, the future Father of Modern Rocketry reminded the audience that "It is impossible to say what is impossible, for the dream of yesterday is the hope of today, and the reality of tomorrow."

FOR THE LOVE OF THE GAME

Peter Gray

Peter Gray loved baseball more than life. He grew up playing sandlot ball and was the best hitter on the block. As a young man, he played semi-pro baseball and then moved on to the major leagues for just one short season. During those few months, Gray so distinguished himself that they installed his glove in the Baseball Hall of Fame at Cooperstown, New York.

Gray's skill notwithstanding, he would never have had the opportunity to play major league baseball had it not been for World War II and the fact that the rosters of most teams had been drained by the draft. One by one, the stars went off to war, and the second stringers left behind were pulled up from the farm clubs.

Pete knew that this was his big chance, and he kept knocking at the door. Finally his persistence paid off, and the St. Louis Browns signed him up to play outfield. It was a glorious day on April 18, 1945, when Peter Gray put on a Brown's uniform and stepped up to bat against the Detroit Tigers. Finally he was realizing his boyhood dream.

Pete went one for four that day and did himself proud on defense as well. The Browns defeated the Tigers 7-1, so all told; he enjoyed a pretty solid start in the Majors.

Gray went on to play in 77 games that season. He got 51 hits for a .218 batting average. He hit six doubles and two triples, while striking out just eleven times. Then in September 1945, it was all over, both the war and Peter's major league baseball career. The veterans were coming home, and his services were no longer needed.

When they came to ask him if they could have his glove for Cooperstown, Pete didn't mind. He knew it had special significance, and if he couldn't be inducted, at least his glove would be there.

And what was it that made Peter Gray's glove so special? The answer was plain to anyone who ever saw him play. It had been specially made for Pete because he only had one arm!

Having lost his right limb just above the elbow in an accident when he was a young lad, Peter learned to use his left hand. He had a shoemaker fit him with a glove that allowed him to handle grounders and fly balls with ease. Then he just bid his time.

Peter Gray died in 2002, a much admired, yet humble man. "I just signed eight dozen baseballs for someone," he told a reporter. "They remember me even though I'm nobody special."

In today's self-seeking climate of professional sports, it is nice to remember that there once was a time when the country had a man who would have given his right arm just to play baseball.

HOW THELMA
HIT THE BIG TIME

There was nothing in the early life of Thelma Catherine to indicate that she would ever be famous. By any reasonable standard, she should never have made it to the top, but she did. When her family moved to Southern California, the talent scouts "discovered" her. The doors to fame and fortune then opened wide for Thelma, and she walked through them and onto a totally unforeseen, worldwide stage.

Thelma was born in 1912 in Nevada, the daughter of a struggling, alcoholic miner. When her parents moved to Southern California, her lot in life improved a little, but not enough to keep her from having to work to help keep food on the table. She picked vegetables after school to help the family.

When she was thirteen years old, her mother died of cancer, and her father's drinking bouts became longer and more frequent. Within three years, he drank himself to death, and Thelma was left to face the world alone.

For awhile she worked as a cleaning lady in a bank at night while she attended Fullerton College in the daytime. She supplemented her income by doing a variety of odd jobs until she graduated. Then Dame Fortune smiled on Thelma when a talent scout saw her on the campus of the University of Southern California.

Thelma's model-like looks and her freshness got her a screen test. Before she knew it, she found herself in the movies. She would never again do cleaning or work in the fields for a living. Thelma Catherine was moving toward a special kind of stardom.

Her first role came in the 1935 classic, *Becky Sharp*, in which she worked with Miriam Hopkins. Then came *Dancing Pirate*, with Frank Morgan, *Small Town Girl*, with Janet Gaynor and Andy Devine, and *The Great Ziegfeld*, with William Powell. No doubt about it, by the late 1930s, Thelma was on her way to fame but not in the way she expected. When she decided to add live theater performances to her credits, her acting career went in a strange direction.

In 1938, Thelma decided to audition for a part with a local acting troupe, and that's where she met the man who stole her heart. Although he lacked her talent, he was nevertheless cast for a part opposite Thelma. He may not have been much of a thespian, but it took him only a few months to persuade her to give up acting and become his wife. When she said yes and turned her back on Hollywood, Thelma Catherine took on the role for a lifetime.

For you see, the man who swept Thelma Catherine (Pat) Ryan off her feet was none other than Richard Milhous Nixon, who would one day carry his wife to real fame when he became the President of the United States. In a surprising twist in time, Pat Nixon left Hollywood and walked onto the stage of history to play a role that made her parts in the movies pale by comparison. For better or for worse, Thelma had arrived.

Thelma Catherine (Pat) Ryan Nixon

JOHN JACOB ASTOR MAKES A FATAL CHOICE

John Jacob Astor, the great grandson of the first John Jacob Astor of Rocky Mountain fur trading fame, was born with a silver spoon in his mouth. As an heir to the Astor millions, almost every eye in America was on the young man. If the public scrutiny had been confined to his business career, that would have been fine. However, when the press began to meddle in his private affairs, Astor took umbrage, and it wound up costing him his life.

After a period of traveling abroad, in 1891, Astor returned to the United States to manage the family fortune. On May 1 of that year, he married Ava Willing of Philadelphia. Not yet thirty years old, Astor then proceeded to put his own stamp on his family's history.

In 1894 he wrote a semi-scientific novel, Journey to Other Worlds and became a dilettante inventor. Three years later Astor built the Astoria Hotel, which adjoined the Waldorf Hotel, built by William Waldorf Astor, his cousin. The new complex became known as the Waldorf-Astoria.

When the Spanish-American War broke out, he became a lieutenant colonel on the staff of General Levi P. Morton. He stunned the nation by placing his own yacht, the Nourmahal, at the disposal of the U.S. government and equipped it with a battery of artillery.

Astor also played roles in two films, "President McKinley's Inspection of Camp Wikoff" and "Colonel John Jacob Astor, Staff and Veterans of the Spanish American War," in which he played himself. By the turn of the century his name had become a household word. Then he began to have marital problems, and life hit a sour note.

In 1909 John Jacob Astor IV divorced Ava Willing Astor. Two

John Jacob Astor

years later he scandalized the nation by marrying eighteen year-old Madeleine Force, who was one year younger than his son, Vincent. So vehement was the public reaction to the respectability of Astor's actions that he decided to take his young bride abroad to escape the gossip at home. They traveled all over Europe and the Middle East, and were having the time of their lives beyond the spotlight of public scrutiny. Then in the spring of 1912 they learned that Madeleine was pregnant, so they decided to go home.

The Astors made their way to Cherbourg and boarded a ship bound for New York. The name of the vessel was the Titanic.

Madeleine survived the disaster at sea, but her husband was counted among the fatalities. They found his body on April 22, and he was brought to New York City for burial. He had lived a charmed life for forty-seven years, and had it not been for the chain of events that followed his marriage to Madeleine, he might have reached a ripe, old age.

If the storm of criticism which descended upon him at the time of his marriage had not been so unsettling, the couple would not have left New York and would have missed the Titanic.

If Madeleine had not become pregnant while they were abroad, they would not have come home when they did and would have missed the Titanic, or if his great grandfather had not made that fortune trapping beaver, he might have been just an ordinary citizen whose morals interested nobody, and he would have missed the Titanic.

Fate does choose its victims strangely.

IN DEFENSE OF JOE McCARTHY

Senator Joe McCarthy

They called him "Tail Gunner Joe," in derision, claiming that he was never in combat during World War II. They assailed his search for communists in government as a "witch-hunt", and they wrote columns about his alcoholism. There can be no doubt about it; the press had no respect for the tactics of Senator Joseph McCarthy. By the time of his censure by the United States Senate in 1954, McCarthy's name had become synonymous with gutter politics. That's what made the actions of one of America's most prominent and progressively thinking families so inexplicable. They apparently loved the hate-monger.

It probably surprised no one that the patriarch of the family took a shine to Joe McCarthy. Neither of them could be placed in the "pure as the driven snow" category. However, when it came to the old man's children, that was another matter. They were all highly educated and well endowed with a fervent sense of *noblesse oblige*. One would have thought that if there was any place where McCarthy would feel uncomfortable it would be in this family's living room. Surprisingly this was not the case.

On any number of occasions, Senator Joe McCarthy was invited to be a weekend guest of the family, and on such occasions he regaled his hosts with stories of his latest tilting at windmills. Presidents Truman and Eisenhower were soft on communism. George Marshall was a traitor to his country. The State Department was filled with pinkos and saboteurs. On and on the Senator went as if he were preaching to the choir.

The family responded to the Senator's tirades with affection. McCarthy dated two of the patriarch's daughters, and one of his sons asked McCarthy to act as godfather of his first child. Later, this same son walked out on a banquet speech by Edward R. Murrow because of the newsman's anti-McCarthy telecast the previous year.

Another son, who himself had won a seat in the United States Senate, performed a similar act at the 100th Anniversary of the Harvard Spree Club dinner. It seems the speaker likened Joseph McCarthy to the Soviet Spy, Alger Hiss, whereupon the son jumped to McCarthy's defense. He rose to his feet and shouted, "How dare you couple the name of a great American patriot with that of a traitor." He then stomped out of the building.

No, America couldn't figure it out. While most everyone else was vilifying the Senator and denouncing McCarthyism, his friends at Hyannis port, Massachusetts, were hopping to his defense.

For you see, it was the family of Joseph Kennedy, Sr. who embraced Senator Joe McCarthy while he was creating havoc in the United States Senate. It was Eunice and Pat who dated him. It was RFK who asked him to be godfather to his firstborn, and it was JFK who called him an American patriot.

By some strange twist in time, the redbaiting antics of Joe McCarthy found a home at Camelot while the rest of the country was holding him at arms' length.

TEDDY ROOSEVELT AND THE SHAH OF IRAN

Kermit Roosevelt

Everybody remembers President Theodore Roosevelt as the man whose pet proverb was "Speak softly and carry a big stick." So potent was TR's admonition to the nation that fifty years later, the government of the United States tried to revive his "Big Stick" policy by turning to the one man who remembered it best.

In 1953, Iran was in a state of turmoil. The Shah had been reduced to a mere figurehead, and Mohammed Mossadegh, the left-leaning Prime Minister, had taken charge. This caused considerable concern in the U.S. because Mossadegh threatened to snatch control of Iranian oil from the West. The State Department made no secret of its feeling that the Prime Minister had to go, but it had to be handled with forceful finesse, so it turned to a CIA agent who had a special fondness for "Big Stick" diplomacy.

The CIA man was dispatched to Iran where he met secretly with the Shah and told him that the "Mossadegh problem" had to be solved. When the puppet ruler inquired as to how this was to be accomplished, the agent answered, "By speaking softly and carrying a big stick." At first the Shah wavered, but when he saw the CIA agent at work, he relented.

In the first days of the coup, its success was far from certain. Crowds who were loyal to Mossadegh rioted so violently in the streets that the Shah fled the country and took refuge in Baghdad. In doing so, however, he reckoned without the tenacity of the CIA agent who was driven by "Big Stick" tactics. He enlisted the support of the army with American dollars, and Iranian soldiers then became the CIA's "big stick."

After Mossadeqh's key supporters were done away with, the CIA agent gradually persuaded the commanders of army units to show themselves on the streets at the head of their units and to face down the pro-Mossadegh mobs. The Prime Minister and officials loyal to him were arrested, and on August 19, just three days after his flight, the Shah was able to return in triumph to his capital, where he later expressed his heartfelt gratitude to the CIA man.

"I owe my throne to God, my people, my army--and to you," sobbed a grateful Shah of Iran to the CIA agent in August 1953. All of that was probably true, but the Shah left out one important factor in his victory: the "Big Stick" policy of Theodore Roosevelt. It had been transported to Iran by the CIA agent, who just happened to be none other than Kermit Roosevelt, the grandson of the President who had coined the phrase, "Speak softly and carry a big stick." In Iran, the younger Roosevelt proved that he had learned his lesson well.

THE ARMY UNLEASHES A SECRET WEAPON ON BOSTON

On the evening of November 28, 1942, the Coconut Grove Ball Room in Boston was packed with dancers and revelers. People were trying to forget that America was at war. Before the night was over, however, tragedy would strike the nightclub, and because the United States was at war, scores of lives would be saved. The army had a secret weapon, and it would use it in the aftermath of the holocaust in Boston.

It was a little before Midnight, when fire broke out in the crowded ballroom, leaving in its wake a sea of death and destruction. Smoke, flames, and the sheer panic that swept through the crowd, pushed the death toll to almost 500!

After sorting the injured from the dead and dying, the doctors at the Boston City and Massachusetts General hospitals were faced with a deluge of causalities such as is seldom seen. It was a grim, heartbreaking situation that called for extraordinary measures, so the medical authorities turned to the military. They knew that down in Rahway New Jersey, the Army had been working on a secret weapon, but it had never been put to the test.

Once the decision was made to appeal to the Army, action came fast. Long-distance wires hummed with the exchange of official O.K's, and in Rahway an unpretentious coupe headed silently into the night from the chemical research laboratories of Merck & Company. As the gates of the great factory clanged behind it, a police escort swung into line, and with sirens screaming, the convoy headed northward.

Before dawn the procession arrived at the gates of the Massachusetts General Hospital. The driver of the coupe, worn and red-eyed from the strain, carried an armload of innocent-looking packages, treating them as gingerly as if they were concentrated dynamite. He handed them over to the waiting physicians. The doctors extracted the glass ampules from the boxes with a touch of reverence. Inside each container a brown powder sluiced around like sand in an egg timer. Now the army would put its secret weapon to the test.

They made a solution out of the brown powder and

chose the worst of the injured from the Boston fire. Over burned surfaces and into veins they poured the solution, and then they waited.

A tight lid of security was clamped on the army's involvement in the tragedy, but one by one, the medical bigwigs who were charged with advising the Army's Surgeon General, slipped into Boston quietly to watch. After reviewing several cases, they were convinced. They returned to their Pullman cars and headed for Washington to inform the government that the weapon had performed beautifully.

The army had intended to maintain the secrecy of their weapon, but it was a futile effort. The news was just too big to keep. After the Coconut Grove fire, Washington broke its silence and announced that the secret weapon that had been so successful was a new medicine that had been created to fight bacteria. It would make sulfa drugs appear as outmoded as the horse and buggy, and its name was penicillin.

THE GOVERNOR WHO COULDN'T WIN

William C. Marland

The man's life was an unusual American success story. He was born into poverty, worked his way through college, and became the highest elected official in his state. As Governor he worked indefatigably for the people and against special interests. Then something happened in 1956, and his life turned sour. That's why the nation gasped on March 12, 1965, when they read the Chicago Tribune. People could not believe what they were being told.

During his first days as Governor, he had done the unthinkable by presenting the state legislature with a proposal to tax the coal industry. As might have been expected, legislators went running for cover. No politician ever took on the coal industry in West Virginia and survived. The bill never made it out of the legislature, and his administration never recovered.

The young Governor tried to redeem himself by bringing diversified industry to his state, but all to no avail. By 1956, he was out of a job, and as the old saying goes, "out of sight, out of mind." Almost overnight, he dropped off the political radar screen, and was nowhere to be found until that Tribune article came out on March 12, 1965.

It was an unbelievable story. For some reason, a reporter was visiting the basement of the YMCA that day, and while he was there, he spotted a man in a cab driver's uniform sitting on a bunk. The newsman didn't have to take a second look. The man sitting there before him, eating fried chicken out of a bag, was none other than William C. Marland, the former Governor of West Virginia.

After he lost his reelection bid in 1956, Marland dropped out of society. He drifted to the slums of Chicago and rarely drew a sober breath for four years. Then something turned him around, and he went on the wagon. He got a job driving a taxi and took up residence in the YMCA.

Marland's story gripped the heart of the nation, and offers of employment came rolling in. Old political cronies sought him out to offer him succor, and for awhile it looked as if Governor Marland was going to experience a political resurrection.

Then just as his life was about to take another miraculous turn, bad news came. Fate was not going to give William C. Marland a happy ending. Just months after the world rediscovered him, Marland was diagnosed with cancer of the pancreas. He died in November 1965, eight months after leaving the taxicab company.

Today in West Virginia, William C. Marland is most often remembered as the "taxicab governor." It is a sad commentary that this young executive is not also remembered for his own brand of bravery, daring to take on the coal companies and battling the demons of alcohol. He came as close to a victory as was possible on both fronts.

THE KING, THE KAISER, AND THE CZAR

England's Queen Victoria set a longevity record for British Monarchs. After ascending the throne in 1837, she ruled for sixty-four years until her death in 1901. During that time, the British Empire reached its zenith, and such was her influence that she gave the period a name—the Victorian age. If only she could have lived a little longer, her family might not have become dysfunctional, and we might have avoided World War I.

Thirteen years after they laid Queen Victoria to rest, England found itself in the middle of a ferocious war. Nationalistic paranoia had seized the countries of Europe, and every head of state constantly looked over his borders to see what was going on in his neighbor's back yard. As a result, a dangerous system of alliances emerged which eventually led to a worldwide bloodletting over the assassination of the Archduke Franz Ferdinand in Sarajevo.

Each side had a number of allies, but three nations bore the heaviest burden in the combat of World War I. Two of them, England and Russia were on one side and Germany was on the other.

All three were old-fashioned monarchies. Russia was ruled by Czar Nicholas II. Kaiser Wilhelm II controlled Germany, and George V was King of England.

For the first three years of the war, hundreds of thousands died, and the front lines didn't shift more than ten miles in either direction during that time. Then in 1917, as the combatants shed oceans of blood on the battlefields, the tide began to turn when two things happened. First the Russians revolted, dethroned their Czar, and dropped out of the war. Second, the United States entered the conflict on the side of Britain and France. From that point on, it was just a matter of time until the outcome was settled. Germany and her allies lost the war.

When the armistice took effect on November 11, 1918, earth-shattering changes rattled Europe. The Russians executed Czar Nicholas and his family, and Kaiser Wilhelm was forced to abdicate his throne and flee to Holland where he spent the rest of his life in exile. In the meantime, England's King George lost a considerable portion of his power to the people. Monarchies in the western world would never again lead their subjects to war. Too many had been cut off in the flower of youth, and it all would have been so unnecessary if only Queen Victoria had been there to ameliorate the situation.

Through the power of her personality, she could have brought the quarreling King, Kaiser, and Czar together before it was too late. She could have urged them to remember who they were and whom they represented. She could have counseled them to be respectful of their common heritage and pointed out that blood was thicker than water.

For you see, this triumvirate of fighting monarchs during World War I belonged to the same family. They had all been destined to share a grandmother. By some strange twist in time, King George V of England, Czar Nicholas II of Russia, and Kaiser Wilhelm II of Germany were all first cousins—the grandsons of the beloved and universally respected Queen Victoria!

THE MAN WHO NEVER, NEVER, NEVER GAVE UP

Young Winston Churchill

The son was destined to become a world leader, but in the beginning he couldn't even please his own father. His first two attempts to get into preparatory school failed, and when he was finally admitted, his academic performance left a lot to be desired.

The father made little effort to conceal his lack of confidence in the young lad's abilities. He once wrote that his son "lacked cleverness, knowledge, and any capacity for settled work." As the boy grew up, it appeared on the surface that his father's analysis was correct, and by the eve of World War II, everybody agreed that he just couldn't get it together. Then Adolf Hitler came along and gave him one more chance.

His first opportunity to prove himself to his family came when they secured for him a seat in Parliament and later the First Lord of the Admiralty during World War I.

Frustrated by the stalemate in Belgium and France, as head of the British Navy, he concocted a plan to outflank the Central Powers by sending his forces to the Mediterranean to open up access to the Black Sea. The entire Gallipoli operation, as it was known, was a galling failure, and the son had to resign in disgrace.

He might have remained a national pariah had not the Conservative Prime Minister given him another chance. He put him in charge of Great Britain's money as Chancellor of the Exchequer. For reasons that are a bit muddled, the son returned his country to the gold standard, which by the 1930s was a financial disaster. Once more he snatched defeat from the jaws of victory and was forced to admit failure and miscalculation again.

With that he threw himself into the debate over self-government for India. As an incurable romantic who cherished the memory of Great Britain's imperial history, he staunchly opposed loosening the political ties between England and India, preferring instead to perpetuate the colonial status of the sub-continent. Once more he allowed his heart to rule his mind, and his political stock tumbled even further.

For the next few years he yelled and screamed against the Bolsheviks and the Fascists, although no one seemed to listen. Then Adolf Hitler became the dictator of Germany, and he got yet another chance.

Germany rearmed, and the British leaders did nothing. Germany reoccupied the Rhineland, and the British leaders did nothing. Hitler grabbed Czechoslovakia and Austria, and the British leaders did nothing. The final straw came when the Nazis dismembered Poland. Now the British people prepared to face facts, and the fact was they needed a strong leader to replace the pusillanimous sycophants who were promoting appeasement. That is when they turned to one of the country's biggest failures, Winston Churchill.

Whatever Churchill's earlier shortcomings as a student and a politician, in 1940, he turned out to be the man for the times. His bulldog tenacity held the British together until help came from the United States and the Fascists were defeated. The people had chosen well, notwithstanding the fact that their choice to face Hitler had been a failure for the better part of his life.

HOW AMERICA BEAT FRANCE AT THE WORLD'S FAIR

In 1893 the organizers of the Chicago World's Fair were on the horns of a dilemma. They were under tremendous pressure to outdo the Paris World's Fair of 1889, but try as they might, they couldn't come up with anything that would rival the Eiffel Tower. Then along came that creative little bridge builder from Pittsburgh. His idea sent everyone spinning.

Gustave Eiffel had built his tower for the Paris Fair of 1889 to honor the 100th anniversary of the French Revolution, and in 1893 it stood as a proud reminder to the French that they had done what a world's fair was supposed to do—capture the imagination of the planet. That, of course, sent the Americans scrambling for an exhibit that was bigger and better.

Finding something that would do the job was a major hurdle for architect Daniel H. Burnham, who was in charge of selecting a project for the Chicago World's Fair that would put the French in their place. As early as 1891, he complained at an engineer's banquet about having found nothing that "met the expectations of the people." Fortunately for Burnham and the Fair, sitting among the audience that day was the owner of a firm that had lots of experience with iron and steel. During the dinner, he was hit with an inspiration and scribbled a design on a napkin and gave it to the befuddled architect.

When Burnham saw the drawing, he wondered out loud if it was really doable. When he was assured that it was indeed possible, the architect authorized the project, and the bridge builder went to work.

First he had to construct two 140-foot steel towers which were then connected by a 45-foot axle. After that came the hard part. He built a large wheel, which had a diameter of 250 feet and a circumference of 825 feet. This wheel section was then fitted up with thirty-six wooden cars, each of which held up to sixty riders each. Finally the whole affair was hooked to the axle between the two towers. Then two 1000-horsepower reversible engines were connected to the wheel, and presto, Chicago had the world's largest carnival ride. Now all they had to do was to name it, and that part came easily.

For you see, that bridge builder who conceived of the idea two years prior was none other than George W. Ferris, the owner of the G.W.G. Ferris & Company, which inspected and tested metals for railroads and bridges. What else could Ferris' contraption be called than the Ferris Wheel?

In an unexpected twist in time, not only did George Ferris save the day for the Chicago Fair, he set the pace for future entrepreneurs. After 1893, no respectable theme park or carnival could be caught without a Ferris Wheel, and all because one little fellow had the courage to think out of the box—or perhaps the circle.

IN PRAISE OF
THOMAS CRAPPER

It is a widely held and much circulated belief that the flush toilet came from the inventive mind of one Thomas Crapper. It has been said that the British subject answered the call of Victorian England for a method of removing sticky deposits from the porcelain on toilets. This claim, however, has recently been examined and found wanting. Several scholars of British sanitation flatly deny that Crapper had anything to do with inventing the flush toilet, and they lay the blame for the error at the pen of the plumber's biographer, whose wit propagated the myth.

There can be no doubt that Crapper was a real person and a high quality plumber. In point of fact, he did garner a number of plumbing patents and even supplied toilets for King Edward VII. It is also true that he founded Crapper and Company Ltd., but contrary to popular opinion, he did not invent the flush toilet. .

Apparently that device was not a single invention; rather, it simply evolved in stages. The first patent for a flushing toilet was issued to Alexander Cummings in 1775. Then in 1778, one Joseph Bramah was issued a patent on an improved toilet and sold over 6,000 of them over the next two decades.

What Thomas Crapper did was imply in his company's advertisements that he was the originator of the flush toilet. That's how the rumor began, and over the years it gathered momentum, until Wallace Reyburn cemented it in the public mind as fact when he wrote Thomas Crapper's biography.

You see, citing material supplied by Crapper's great-niece, Reyburn declared unequivocally that his subject did indeed invent the flush toilet.

After the publication of Reyburn's tome, there was no doubt in the pubic mind as to the contribution of Thomas Crapper to civilized society. In an incredulous twist in time, who could doubt it after reading such convincing evidence as Reyburn had gathered under the title, "Flushed with Pride."

NEGLECT OF THE TROOPS PROMPTS A "ROUND ROBIN" REVIEW

The Maine Enters Havana Harbor

For a few months in 1898, the United States and Spain fought what some politicians characterized as a "splendid little war." The conflict officially began in April and ended in August with relatively few casualties to the victorious American forces. Actually it was a cakewalk as far as wars go, but one newly commissioned Colonel didn't see it that way.

Notwithstanding the fact that jingoistic newspaper accounts of the supremacy of U.S. soldiers saturated the country, if the Spaniards had held out just a little longer, the American army might have melted away--especially in Cuba, and that's what made the Colonel mad.

The shooting there had no sooner ceased than he began to make trouble. He pointed out that when they had boarded troop transports in Tampa, Florida, bound for Cuba, they had to wait in the broiling June sun for a week before getting under way.

Then when they finally did arrive in Cuba, 17,000 soldiers disembarked wearing heavy woolen underwear and uniforms designed for subzero operations against the Indians. Their rations throughout the fighting consisted of "odorous canned meat," which the men called "embalmed beef."

By the time the August armistice was signed, malaria, typhoid, dysentery, and yellow fever had become so severe that hundreds were incapacitated. That's when the Colonel decided to do something.

At some risk of being accused of insubordination, he became the ringleader in making "round robin" demands on Washington D.C. They read in part, "We...are of the unanimous opinion...that the army is disabled and must be moved now. The persons responsible for preventing such a move will be responsible for the unnecessary loss of many thousands of lives."

When officials in the nation's capital received the "round robin" demands, they read it with a sense of wonderment. Each of the signatories had signed the document in circular form around all four edges of the paper, hence its name, "round robin." This made it impossible to determine precisely who was responsible for the document, but one name stood out from all the rest.

There in one corner was a name they all recognized. Before the war he had been the Assistant Secretary of the Navy. During the war he had been commissioned a Colonel and had led the now famous charge up San Juan Hill near Santiago. The authorities eyed one another. You see, they pondered the signature of Colonel Theodore Roosevelt of Rough Rider renown.

It comes as no surprise that more than 25,000 men were quickly transferred out of Cuba for New York. In a persistent twist in time, Teddy Roosevelt had made his point with his "round robin" document, and if he had not maintained absolute anonymity, he at least was no more than first among equals.

CHICANERY AT THE SMITHSONIAN INSTITUTION

The Flyer in the Smithsonian

The Smithsonian Institution has been the official caretaker of American History since 1846, when President James K. Polk signed the Act, which established it as such. Since that time the Smithsonian has valiantly stood guard over the truth of America's past, with one notable exception. In 1914, Dr. Charles D. Walcott set about to rob the Wright Brothers of their rightful place in the history of flight and wound up paying a painful price.

Wilbur and Orville Wright made their historic flight at Kitty Hawk, North Carolina on December 17, 1903, and in so doing, they beat out Samuel P. Langley for the honor and distinction of demonstrating the world's first successful airplane.

While the Wright Brothers had been conducting their experiments with flight, Langley had also been working feverishly to become the first to build a machine that could fly like a bird. By December 8, 1903, he was ready. As Wilber and Orville prepared to launch their "Flyer," at Kitty Hawk, Langley set about to attempt to fly his "Aerodrome" off of a houseboat anchored in the middle of the Potomac River.

Langley's attempt was an unmitigated disaster. The "Aerodrome" plummeted from the housetop straight down into the water. Almost overnight the pioneer aviator became the butt of a national joke, and his aircraft was dubbed "Langley's Folly." Meanwhile the Wright Brothers captured the praise of the country with their successful venture in North Carolina and went into the history books, or so they thought. Little did they know that Langley had a good friend in high places.

In 1914, Walcott, the Secretary of the Smithsonian Institution, brought Langley's "Aerodrome" to Washington D.C. and put it on display, complete with a placard which identified it as the world's first heavier-than-air craft. Langley had been his predecessor at the Smithsonian, and he wanted his friend to have the honor that rightfully belonged to the Wright Brothers. By that time, Wilbur had died, and no one expected Orville to raise any objections.

It didn't take long, however, for Walcott to regret his attempt to rewrite history. When Orville discovered the official fraud, he designed a plan to bring the Smithsonian to its knees. It took over thirty years, but America's national museum finally acknowledged its mistake and put the Wright Brothers' "Flyer" on display in the Smithsonian's Arts and Industries Building with the credit it deserved.

And where had the "Flyer" been all those years? It had been on display in Great Britain! You see, when Orville Wright learned of the chicanery at the Smithsonian, he decided to take the "Flyer" out of the country. In a brilliant twist in time, he loaned it to the London Science Museum, and that is where it remained until 1948, the year that Orville Wright died, and justice was finally served.

MAINTAINING THE DIGNITY OF CHEF BOYARDEE

1959 Advertisement

    Hector Boiardi came to America from his native Italy and lived out the American dream. Not only did he work hard and make a fortune, he created such a sense of loyalty among his followers that no one, not even Jerry Seinfeld, could poke fun at his work with impunity. When the famous comedian tried to make people laugh at Hector's handicraft, he ran into a brick wall of opposition.

    Hector Boiardi came to New York in 1914 and landed a job in the Ritz Carlton as a cook. A few years later, he moved to Cleveland to become the Hotel Winton's chef. That was where he developed his soon-to-be famous spaghetti dinners, and soon after that people forgot about his first name and just called him "Chef Boyardee."

    Chef Boyardee's special recipe for spaghetti sauce seduced the public's palate so effectively that in 1924, he opened his own restaurant. When demand for the special sauce whipped his customers into a culinary lather, he enlarged his business and began an assembly line production of his popular invention.

By the 1940s, Chef Boyardee had aroused the attention of the nation, and even the government joined the clamor for his products by engaging his company to supply the military with pre-packaged food, which included his new "Beef-a-Roni" specialty. It was this Boyardee item that would later cause Seinfeld such a problem.

In June 1985, Hector Boiardi died, but Chef Boyardee lived on through his then famous food products. American Home Foods took over the reins of his company and carefully guarded his secret recipes. Little did they dream that they would one day have to step in to put a halt to what they considered to be a demeaning use of Beef-a-Roni by the Seinfeld television show.

You see, Seinfeld had written an episode in 1996, which he entitled "The Rye." During the filming, Kramer, one of the show's characters, was supposed to feed a healthy helping of Beef-a-Roni to a horse. Now at first blush, there was nothing objectionable about that, but when the script called for the horse to experience a powerful release of flatulence, the folks at Chef Boyardee drew the line. They weren't about to allow people to think that Chef Boyardee caused the animal such gastric distress, so they called a halt to the show.

Of course that left the ball squarely in Seinfeld's court, and he pulled a fast one. He had Kramer go ahead and feed the horse, but not with Beef-a-Roni. In a sly twist in time, he gave the animal something called Beef-a-Reeno, and in the end, the horse performed the required digestive function right on cue.

So everyone was satisfied. No one was able to link Beef-a-Roni with anything uncouth. Hector's dignity was maintained, and Seinfeld had his show. Only one thing was missing. No one knows for sure how it really affected the horse.

THE DAY THE U.S. GOVERNMENT LOOKED A GIFT HORSE IN THE MOUTH

Norman Rockwell's Freedom From Want

Every year as Americans make ready for Thanksgiving, the ritual of families gathered around a bountiful table, complete with a turkey dinner and all of the trimmings is reenacted. Although it had been a national tradition for years, the scene was first illustrated in 1942 by Norman Rockwell in his now famous "Four Freedoms" posters. Rockwell's inspiration for the artwork came from President Franklin Roosevelt and eventually took the country by storm, but if a group of government minions had had their way, they never would have seen the light of day.

Rockwell got the idea for his "Four Freedoms" paintings after listening to FDR give his State of the Union address in 1941. The President brought the nation to its feet with his proclamation that he looked forward to a time in which freedom of speech, freedom of worship, freedom from want, and freedom from fear prevailed throughout the world. Rockwell was so taken by Roosevelt's oratory that he decided to illustrate the four freedoms.

Norman Rockwell labored on these paintings for 6 months. He lost 15 pounds and many nights' sleep, but when he was finished, he had created some of the greatest masterpieces of his entire career. That's when The Saturday Evening Post stepped in and published the paintings. The public response was so great that 25,000 readers ordered sets of Rockwell's prints from the magazine.

Rockwell received over 60,000 letters and postcards offering thanks and encouragement. Included in this number was one letter from the President himself. Roosevelt wrote, "I think you have done a superb job in bringing home to the plain, everyday citizen the plain, everyday truths behind the Four Freedoms... I congratulate you...."

Rockwell's paintings became so popular that they organized a tour to sixteen American cities. Almost a million and a quarter people lined up to appreciate his work in person. That's when the Office of War Information (OWI) did a very strange thing. They appealed to Rockwell for permission to use his Four Freedoms posters to help sell war bonds.

In time Rockwell consented to allow his work to be used by the government, but it took a little convincing. You see, the artist had first offered his posters to the government for use in selling war bonds, but the OWI turned him down! The head of the agency determined that Rockwell's posters just didn't have what it took to inspire people. That's when Rockwell turned to The Saturday Evening Post.

Thus, in a most embarrassing twist in time, the Office of War Information did an about-face and hopped on the Rockwell bandwagon. They printed 2.5 million copies of the paintings that they had earlier rejected and sold $130 million worth of bonds. One has to wonder if prints of Norman Rockwell's "Four Freedoms" every graced the walls of the OWI headquarters.

ONE WRITER'S WORDS BOUNCE BACK TO HAUNT HIM

H.L Mencken

    In the early 1930s, what is known as the Eastern Shore of Maryland was racked with racial violence. Three murder cases resulted in the lynching of two Blacks there, and the famous reporter and social critic, H.L. Mencken, lambasted the vigilantes who took the law into their own hands. However, while the famous writer vilified the entire Eastern Shore, he conveniently forgot that time some years earlier when he wrote words that would now come back to haunt him.

    Mencken first aimed his caustic pen at every resident of Maryland who lived east of Chesapeake Bay and south of Delaware in December of 1931. At issue was the lynching of Mack Williams for killing his boss, Daniel Elliott.

    From his office in the Baltimore Sun, Mencken launched a tirade against the folks on the Eastern Shore. He claimed that the area had been on a moral decline for years. "The Ku Klux Klan...got a firm lodgment in the lower counties of the Shore, and the brutish imbecilities that it propagated are still accepted gravely," Mencken claimed.

    The famous writer went on to charge that "the whole area is a lush stomping ground for knavish politicians, prehensile professional patriots, and whooping soul-savers who have passed the running of things into the hands of ninth-rate men, making the region an Alsatia of morons, which is to say of lynchers."

It didn't take long for folks on the Eastern Shore to answer Mencken. The respectable people there denounced the local atrocities as vociferously as had the Baltimore writer, but at the same time they returned a volley of their own. Someone recovered an article that H.L. had written in 1926, which made him look and sound like one of the very people he was denouncing.

At that time, Mencken had just finished his coverage of the "Scopes Monkey Trial" in which three-time Presidential candidate and perennial loser, William Jennings Bryan, attempted to defend fundamentalist Christianity against the onslaught of the theory of evolution. Such was Mencken's outrage at Bryan that he publicly suggested the latter's demise in a manner that would have made the Williams' lynching look like a lawn party.

Writing with Bryan clearly in mind, Mencken proposed in print a Constitutional amendment which would provide for an unappealing end for every loser in a presidential election. Mencken would haul the unsuccessful candidate (Bryan) up to the top of the Washington Monument on Inauguration Day where he would be "shot, poisoned, strangled, disemboweled, and his carcass thrown into the Potomac River."

The discovery of H.L. Mencken's hate-filled diatribe didn't get the Eastern Shore folks off the hook. No one could deny the horrific lynchings in their neighborhoods. At the same time, however, in a revengeful twist in time, they were able to accomplish the impossible. For a while they were able to leave H.L. Mencken speechless—an unrivalled accomplishment in the literary world.

PANCHO VILLA TO THE RESCUE

The General, his wife, Frances, and their four children had returned briefly to the Presidio in San Francisco before moving to their permanent station at Fort Bliss. Originally, plans had called for the family to travel to Texas together, but Frances had been prevailed upon to speak at a regional reunion of her classmates from Wellesley on August 25, 1915. When she assented to the request, it set the stage for a major tragedy. The General bid his family good-bye and headed east, never to see his wife and daughters again.

The reunion was held on Wednesday, and the next evening Frances entertained guests in the General's quarters, perhaps offering farewells before her planned departure on Friday to join her husband at Fort Bliss. That night, however, fate played its trump card.

Around 4:20 A.M., hot coals in the fireplace spilled out of the grate onto the wooden floor, which had been polished to a high gloss for the previous night's reception. In the next room, Frances' best friend and guest, Ann Boswell, awoke to the sound of crackling wood, already ablaze. Smoke filled her upstairs bedroom as Ann grabbed her two children and took them out onto the porch roof from which they jumped to safety. Then she ran back into the burning building in an attempt to reach Frances—all to no avail.

John J. Pershing

When the fire was extinguished, they found Frances and her four children unconscious near the door. Rescue workers pulled them to the parade ground and made every effort to resuscitate them, but only young Warren survived. His mother and three sisters, Mary, Ann, and Helen, died out on the grass in front of the smoldering building.

The General had just arrived at Fort Bliss when the telegram came. It read, "Wife and three children suffocated in fire at Presidio. Warren in serious condition."

Stunned, he took the first train west from El Paso. When he arrived in San Francisco, he met his father-in-law, Senator Francis E. Warren and rode with him to the Presidio. Looking at the burned-out remains of his quarters, the General could only say, "They had no chance."

After making arrangements for the care of his son, the General returned to Fort Bliss and settled into a deep depression, which might have ended his career if it had not been for Pancho Villa. Three months after the disastrous Presidio fire, the Mexican revolutionary stopped a train in Chihuahua and murdered several Americans. In March 1916, Villa crossed the border and raided the town of Columbus, New Mexico. That's when President Wilson ordered the General to lead his troops on a punitive expedition into Mexico, and that's what brought the grieving man alive again.

For you see that general who lost his wife and daughters in August 1915, was none other than John J. (Black Jack) Pershing. In an ironic twist in time, after his family tragedy he married the Army and became a symbol for dedication to the American military as well as the nation's first five-star general. One wonders how things would have turned out if Pershing had not had Pancho Villa with which to deal at such a crucial time in his life.

OLD WORLD ODDITIES
WITH A TWIST

VENERATION TOOK ITS TOLL

The nine-car train was full and running over with passengers on that day in 1981. Over 1000 people had boarded and were traveling through the northeastern state of Bihar. They were about 250 miles from Calcutta, India.

Outside, monsoon-like conditions were battering the region. Heavy winds and torrential rains buffeted the cars, but they caused no undue alarm. On the inside, everyone was high and dry and looked forward to reaching their destination. There was no way that anyone could have foreseen the nature of the tragedy that was about to engulf them.

The extremely hard rains had swollen the rivers—especially the Baghmati River, and as the train approached the bridge over its waters, the engineer suddenly saw something on the tracks up ahead. As he applied the brakes with all of the force he could muster, it came as no surprise that the cars began to slide on the wet tracks.

The engine and two of the nine cars made it to the other side, but the last seven cars derailed and tumbled down into the river along with its terrified passengers. With its waters so far above normal, the cars quickly sank into the murky waters.

Rescue help was hours away, and by the time they arrived, little could be done for those who had been aboard those last seven cars. Search as they might, the would-be rescuers were transformed into retrievers, and after a multi-day search, only 286 bodies were found, leaving over 300 more that were missing. They would never be recovered.

When authorities finished the last count, they estimated that nearly 600 people lost their lives in the horrific accident.

After completing the body count, the investigators turned to the engineer. Why had he made such a perilous decision? Why did he apply the brakes under conditions that were sure to place the entire train in danger as it crossed the raging waters of the Baghmati? There had to be an answer for his inexplicable action, and most assuredly there was.

Just as the train was approaching the bridge, the horrified engineer had spotted an animal slowly crossing the tracks on the other end of the trestle. He was suddenly thrown on the horns of a terrible dilemma. Where was his loyalty to lie? Should he insure the safety of his passengers by sacrificing the animal on the tracks, or should he follow the dictates of his conscience and do all within his power to avoid hitting the beast?

The engineer chose to save the animal and sacrifice his human cargo, and when he explained this to the authorities, he was completely exonerated. You see the animal that had wandered up on the tracks on that stormy night was a sacred animal to millions of Hindus. In a tragic twist in time, the train engineer made his decision. The fate of the human passengers would have to take second place to an animal that was protected by thousands of years of veneration. Thus did hundreds of people lose their lives because the engineer couldn't bring himself to allow his train to hit a holy cow.

TURKISH DELIGHT IN VIENNA FAILED TO SAVE THE QUEEN

Marie Antoinette

After the Ottoman Turks established their kingdom on the remains of the Byzantine Empire, it didn't take long for them to cast covetous eyes to the West. For 300 years they attempted to add Europe to their conquests, but in 1683, a simple baker turned the tide against them forever. When the fight was finally over, he added insult to injury by rubbing salt in the wounds of the Turkish invaders. He prepared a commemorative culinary delight that made the enemy blush but drew cheers from his countrymen.

The Battle of Vienna began when the Turks decided to dig tunnels under the city walls at night and then pop out to put their European enemies to the sword. It was a brilliant tactic and might have worked if that baker, Peter Wender, had not been so diligent. While he was working in the early morning hours in the basement of his bakery, he heard strange noises coming from inside his walls. The baker hurriedly notified the authorities who discovered the Turks and drove them off. Almost overnight, Peter Wender became a national hero.

For his part, Wender so enjoyed the attention he was getting that he decided to go one better. He would create a special pastry in honor of the occasion. Using the crescent on the Turkish flag as a model, Peter made a roll in the same shape, and soon a tradition was born. It became fashionable for the Viennese to have Wender's pastry with their morning coffee, and every time they took a bite out of the crescent, it had the symbolic effect of thumbing their noses at the Turks. Soon a tradition was born and spread throughout the Holy Roman Empire. Then along came Marie Antoinette, who created an international market for Peter Wender's roll.

It just so happened that the future Queen of France was born in Vienna and grew up eating Peter Wender's crescent shaped delicacy. In 1770, the Hapsburg princess left her native Austria for France to marry the Bourbon prince who became Louis XVI. Among the treasures that she brought from home was the recipe for the crescent shaped Wender's rolls. Within months the French royal baker was duplicating Peter Wender's pastry, only by now it had a new name.

You see, when Marie Antoinette introduced the Viennese crescent roll to the Parisians, they called it a croissant. In a delicious twist in time, Peter Wender's creation became universally popular and millions of people all over the world enjoy his handiwork to this very day. It's too bad that the Queen didn't offer the starving poor of France a croissant instead of telling them to "eat cake." She might have kept her head.

BOBBY LIVES ON

The London Police

Many things in modern America are taken for granted, and not the least of these is the protection provided by local police. So ubiquitous is their presence that it is commonly imagined that they have been around for centuries. Such, however, is not the case. The world's first organized police force is less than 200 years old. It was born in London, and its members were—and still are—called "Bobbies" for a very good reason.

Before the appearance of "Bobbies" in London, most crime was combated by the local constabulary, citizen patrols, or private guards like the Thames River Police, created by the powerful West India Company to deter thefts along the wharves. Soon, however, crime grew so rampant that the government moved to meet the crisis. In 1829 a Member of Parliament, who would one day become Prime Minister, proposed the establishment of the world's first permanent city police force. He sponsored the "Metropolitan Police Act," and secured his place in history when his "Bobbies" took to the streets.

At first the "Bobbies" were assigned only to the outer parts of London and did not work in the mile-square downtown part of the city. They were not popular right away and were often jeered while on patrol, but they persevered. Before long their success at crime fighting won them the respect that was needed from the man on the street.

Bobbies were given the unique responsibility of crime detection and prevention. Their founder wanted them to do more than just show up after someone was victimized and haphazardly attempt to solve the crime; therefore, he put them on "beats" where they could readily recognize suspicious things out of place and help deter wrongdoing.

By 1839, the public was won over, and the "Bobbies" were assigned to begin patrols in the city proper. Twenty years later Parliament went further and mandated that police forces be established in the outlying provinces. By this time, police departments in America were forming on the model of the "Bobbies." They adopted many of their procedures but left their name alone. That would be reserved for the London police in honor of the English politician who created them.

Today, the London "Bobbie" is a familiar sight, dressed as he is in his blue suit and tall hat. Everybody knows who he is, for he has become an institution himself. A few citizens even remember the man who created him. They pay homage to him every time they mention the name of those London policemen. For you see that English statesman who came up with the idea of a police force in London was none other than Robert (Bobby) Peel, and in a respectful twist in time, his law-enforcing proteges were given the name "Bobbies." History it seems even honors nicknames.

THE LADY
LEFT A LEGACY

Jennie Jerome Churchill

Jeanette (Jennie) Jerome is remembered for any number of reasons. She was an American who hit the big time in England's high-brow society. She was known for her numerous, extra-marital affairs. She gave birth to an illegitimate son, and she loved to show off the tattoo of a snake, which twined around her left wrist. All things considered, she was definitely a free spirit during the restrictive atmosphere of the Victorian age, but there is one item in her well documented life that is often overlooked. She also made a contribution to the history of libations that will live on forever.

Jennie was born in Brooklyn, New York, with the proverbial silver spoon in her mouth. Her father, Leonard Jerome, was a New York financier who owned and operated the New York Times. In 1874, he took his daughter to London to hobnob with nobility, and she soon found herself pregnant by an English Lord.

After a quick and quiet marriage in the British embassy in Paris, Jennie gave birth to her first child. Six years later, she became the mother of another son, but not by her husband. During those years between the births of her two sons, she allowed no amorous grass to grow under her feet.

She enjoyed the company of Alexandra of Denmark as well as that of her friend's husband, Edward IV. Her other lovers included Count Charles Andreas Kinsky, King Edward VII of the United Kingdom, and King Milan of Serbia. No doubt about it, Jenny Jerome was a very popular woman.

Oddly enough, her husband didn't appear to object to her dalliances, which she continued until his death in 1895. Five years later, at the age of 46, she married George Cornwallis-West, who was 20 years her junior. Jennie was apparently more than the young military officer could handle, so they separated and were divorced in 1914.

Jennie entered matrimony a third time when she wed another man who was 20 years younger than she was. That marriage to Montague Phippen Porch in 1918 lasted until her death three years later.

As is the case with most unconventional personalities, titillating stories about her life ran rife after her death, but one that is rarely repeated today comes from her days in America. The year was 1874, and Jenny was the host of a party celebrating the election of Samuel J. Tilden to the governorship of New York. Jenny wanted the occasion to be unique, so she commissioned a bartender to prepare a special concoction. The drink he came up with was such a success that Jenny named it after the club in which it was born.

You see, Jenny held that 1874 celebration party at the Manhattan Club, and in a convenient twist in time, she called the new drink the "Manhattan" cocktail. Today it is enjoyed by millions who would never dream that it was named by the woman who would one day become the mother of Winston Churchill. The Lady certainly left a legacy.

FAME HAD ITS PRICE

Mary Ann Walker was the daughter of an English locksmith and his wife Caroline. At the time of her birth on August 26, 1845, there was no indication that she would meet the end that she did 43 years later. Her father made a decent living for the family, and she grew up thinking she would marry and live a life free of many of the cares of this world, but this was not to be. By the time she was 40, she had hit rock bottom and lived on the dole in a London poorhouse. However, if riches in this life eluded Mary, at least her death gave her fame.

On January 16, 1864, Mary Ann Walker became the wife of William Nichols, a printer's machinist who provided his family with the usual amenities expected of a working man. They didn't live the life of Riley, but they didn't live hand-to-mouth either. The couple produced five children and was relatively happy until the 1880s. That's when their marriage went on the rocks. William became involved in an extra-marital affair with a nurse and began to drink heavily. Mary Ann answered her husband's infidelity with some of her own. Soon afterwards they separated. Legally required to support his estranged wife, Nichols paid her an allowance of five shillings a week for a year or two, but when Mary moved in with another man, he terminated her allotment. Not long after that, Mary turned to prostitution for a living and to workhouses for a place of abode.

Then came a short interlude when she returned to her father's house, but they quarreled constantly until she left and moved in with a blacksmith. From there things went from bad to worse, as her drinking intensified. By May of 1888, she was living in the Lambeth workhouse and had become a domestic servant. Becoming quickly dissatisfied with the position, she left her employer a month later, stealing clothing worth three pounds, ten shillings during her departure.

At this point, Mary returned to a life of prostitution, and inadvertently into the London limelight. By the summer of 1888, she was living in a Whitechapel lodging house and working the streets. On August 30, lacking the fourpence for a bed, she went out in search of a customer; instead she walked onto the pages of history.

She was last seen in the area, drunk and disoriented. At 3:40 in the morning two men found her mutilated body in front of a gated stable entrance on a backstreet, ironically just two hundred yards from a London Hospital. Her throat had been slashed and her abdomen cut open.

As gruesome as her death was, Mary didn't gain fame right away. It took several more killings that year for the murdered woman to assume some notoriety, for you see, Mary met her end at the hands of the world's most infamous serial killer. In a terrifying twist in time, she became the first victim of London's "Jack the Ripper."

No one knows for sure the identity of "Jack the Ripper," but there is no doubt about who was the first to feel his blade. Poor Mary Walker Nichols slid from the arms of an unsympathetic father to an unfaithful husband, and finally into the hands of a merciless psychopath. Fame did have its price.

PARLIAMENT GOT AN EARFUL

Robert Jenkins lived most of his life at sea. At an early age he took command of a merchant ship, the *Rebecca*, and plied the waters between England and the Caribbean carrying trade goods that created enormous profits for him and his company. Robert would no doubt have become a very wealthy man had it not been for the humiliation he suffered at the hands of a Spanish naval officer who boarded the *Rebecca* and attacked Jenkins. When he unveiled tangible evidence of the barbarism inflicted upon him by his Spanish tormentor, the English Parliament wretched with horror at what they saw and immediately declared war on Spain. While this eight-year conflict put an end to Jenkins' commercial ventures, he did get his revenge.

The *Rebecca* has just gotten under way and was headed for London when it was stopped by a Spanish war ship and boarded. Although the action by the Spanish captain, Juan de Leon Fandino, was not entirely unexpected, his mutilation of Jenkins shocked the English crew to their toes.

Fandino brought the crew of the *Rebecca* on deck and lined them up. As the Spanish captain taunted them for their attempt to monopolize the Caribbean trade, he reserved his most provocative action for Jenkins.

The War of Jenkins' Ear

When the Spanish captain reached Jenkins, he favored him with a special gesture of contempt. He grabbed the English captain by the hair and then drew his sword. Jenkins was left on his knees holding his head in pain and shame. His life had been spared, but his dignity was gone!

On October 19, 1739, Robert Jenkins walked into the hushed chambers of the House of Commons. He wore a bandage around his head, and he carried a small box. A livid Prime Minister, Robert Walpole, introduced Jenkins to the assemblage, and demanded a declaration of war on Spain. For years Great Britain had been forced to endure outrages on the high seas from her European competitors in the race for colonial trade, but his latest episode was too much even for the stoic Englishman.

After recounting the indignities, which the English crown had suffered through King William's War (1689-1697) and Queen Anne's War (1702-1713), Walpole asked that Jenkins be given the floor. Slowly, carefully, and a bit theatrically, Jenkins rose to tell his story, and at the conclusion, he lifted the box he was carrying. With tenderness Jenkins reached inside and pulled out the evidence. Holding out the palm of his hand for all to see, he showed Parliament the dried up, withered ear that Captain Fandino had sliced from his head on the deck of the *Rebecca*.

The members of Parliament recoiled in disgust and then voted to avenge Jenkins by declaring war. In a matter of months, the nations of Europe were once more lined up to do battle. Thus it was that the macabre humiliation of Robert Jenkins pushed England into a declaration of hostilities. Officially the eight-year struggle was called King George's War, but in a patriotic twist in time, its popular name was "The War of Jenkins' Ear." Robert's countrymen were determined to return to him a measure of his self-respect.

OLIVER CROMWELL LOST HIS HEAD

Oliver Cromwell

In 1649, Charles I, King of England, lost his head—literally. With Charles' execution, the man who was most responsible for his demise, Oliver Cromwell, took the reins of power as Lord Protector until his own death in 1658. Two years later, Parliament had a change of heart and invited Charles II, to return to England and restore the monarchy. When this son of the beheaded king came home, one of his first acts was to vindicate his father's murder in such a macabre way that it took three centuries to complete.

King Charles II ordered that Cromwell's remains be exhumed from Westminster Abbey, and four days later, on the anniversary of the execution of Charles I, the Lord Protector hung from the gallows all day long. Then as dusk approached, Cromwell's embalmed body was taken down, and in an ironic twist of fate, his head was cut off.

Thus the beheading of Charles I was avenged by the post-mortem decapitation of Oliver Cromwell and most folks thought that would be the end of it. Little did they know!

History doesn't record with certainty what happened to Cromwell's body, but his head was put on a stake and displayed at Westminster Hall for more than 20 years. At some point after 1684, a strong gale blew it off the pole and a sentry recovered it and kept it in hiding for several years.

The location of Oliver Cromwell's head remained a mystery until 1710, when it was found in a private museum in London. Then it disappeared again until 1770 when one Samuel Russell tried to sell the head to Cromwell's old college, Sidney Sussex—an offer the college refused.

By 1787, Russell found a private buyer named James Cox, who owned his own museum. Later Cox sold Cromwell's head to three brothers, and in 1799 they put the head on exhibition. In 1814, Cromwell's head, minus his torso, was sold once again—this time to Josiah Henry Wilkerson.

The Wilkerson family continued well into the 20th century to own the head. In 1930, Horace Wilkerson agreed to allow scientists full access to their gory possession. In a 100-page text, complete with illustrations, the forensic pathologists firmly concluded that this was indeed Oliver Cromwell's head.

Horace Wilkerson then stored the head in a bank vault, and upon his death, it was once more offered to Sidney Sussex College. This time its fellows accepted, and on February 12, 1960, Oliver Cromwell's head was finally re-buried almost 300 years after it had been dug up from Westminster Abbey.

Thus the act of revenge by Charles II on the body of his father's mortal enemy gave new meaning to "losing one's head." It was one thing to separate a head from the shoulders but quite another story when that head traveled around the countryside for 300 years.

THE GERMAN WHO FOUGHT HIS FAMILY

World War II was raging when William Patrick, a 35 year-old immigrant, walked into the draft office to join the United States Navy. He told the recruiting officer that, although he had a brother serving in the German army, he wanted to fight against Adolf Hitler. He had decided in 1938, to flee Nazi Germany and come to America. By 1944, he was so revolted by the atrocities of the German leader, he was moved to join the Allies in their fight against the Fatherland.

The recruiting officer was a bit taken aback. What would make this man want to leave his family in Germany and join the war against his countrymen? Then when the enlistee put his name on the dotted line, the Navy chief's surprise turned to astonishment. He could not believe his eyes.

William Patrick's incredible story began when he was born in Liverpool, England to a German father and an English mother. The marriage did not last long, and when the couple separated, the father returned to Germany, married again, and began another family. When William was 18, he went to Germany to live with his father and his new family, which now included Heinz, a younger brother.

William was engaged in a variety of jobs in Germany. He worked in a bank and at the Opel car factory. Finally, he found employment as a used car salesman. Then the storm clouds began to gather over Europe, and when Heinz joined the German army, William set out for America.

Once he was safely in the United States, William wrote an article for Look Magazine in which he severely took Adolf Hitler to task. The tirade against the Nazis attracted the attention of William Randolph Hearst, who immediately put the young dissenter on the lecture circuit.

William railed against the Nazis until he had no words left. By 1944, he was ready to "walk the talk," so he took the unusual step of enlisting in the United States military to fight against his own family. Not only would he and his brother be fighting on opposite sides in World War II, William would be doing his best to defeat his own uncle.

For you see, William Patrick was not an average German defector. His father was Alois Hitler, and his uncle was Adolf Hitler. In a unique twist in time, William Patrick Hitler, the disillusioned nephew of the German Dictator found a way to oppose his sadistic kinsman by joining the forces dedicated to his destruction.

Small wonder then that the naval recruiter responded so sarcastically in 1944, when he read William's signature on the enlistment papers. "So your last name is Hitler," he sneered. "Well I'm Rudolf Hess."

William Patrick Hitler

BIBLIOGRAPHY

Aldrich, Lorenzo D. A Journal of the Overland Route to California & theGold Mines. Los Angeles: Dawson's Book Shop, 1950.

Ambrose, Stephen E. Nothing Like it in the World. New York: Simon and Schuster, 2000.

Apostol, Jane. El Alisal, Where History Lingers. Los Angeles: Historical Society of Southern California.

Audubon, John Woodhouse. Audubon's Western Journal, 1849-1850. Tucson, Arizona: The University of Arizona Press, 1984.

Bailey, Thomas A. The American Pageant. Volume I. Boston: D.C. Heath and Company, 1966.

Bailey, Thomas A. The American Pageant. Volume II. Boston: D.C. Heath and Company, 1966.

Bates, Ed Bryant. True Tales of Outlaws & Rogues. Coarsegold, California: .45 Caliber Publishing, 2001.

Berenger, Clara. "The Woman Who Taught Her Children to Be Fools." America: An Illustrated Diary of its Most Exciting Years. Valencia, California: American Family Enterprises, Inc., 1973.

Bernard, Bruce. Century. London: Phaidon Press Limited. 1999.

Bieber, Ralph P. (ed.) The Southwest Historical Series, Vol. VII: Exploring Southwestern Trails 1846-1854. Glendale, California: The Arthur H. Clark Company, 1938.

BIBLIOGRAPHY

Bieber, Ralph P. (ed.) The Southwest Historical Series, Vol. XII: Analytical Index. Glendale, California: The Arthur H. Clark Company, 1943.

Bieber, Ralph P. Southern Trails to California in 1949. Philadelphia: Porcupine Press, 1974.

Billington, Ray Allen. The Far Western Frontier. New York: Harper & Row Publishers, 1956.

Billington, Ray Allen. The Protestant Crusade: 1800-1860. Gloucester, Massachusetts: Holt, Rinehart, & Winston, Inc., 1963.

Billington, Ray Allen. Westward Expansion. New York: The Macmillan Company, 1967.

Botkin, B.A. (ed.). Civil War Treasury of Tales, Legends, & Folklore. New York: Promontory Press, 1960.

Brands, H.W. Andrew Jackson. New York: Doubleday, 2005.

Bruff, J. Goldsborough. Gold Rush. Vol II. New York: Columbia University Press, 1944.

Bryant, Edwin. What I Saw in California. Santa Ana, California: The Fine Arts Press, 1936.

Capps, Benjamin. The Great Chiefs. Alexandria, Virginia: Time-Life Books, 1975.

Caro, Robert A. The Years of Lyndon Johnson: Master of the Senate. New York: Vintage Books, 2002.

Carruth, Gorton. Encyclopedia of American Facts & Dates. New York: Harper & Row, 1987.

BIBLIOGRAPHY

Catton, Bruce. The American Heritage New History of the Civil War. New York: Penguin Books, 1996.

Caughey, John Walton. Gold is the Cornerstone. Berkeley, California: University of California Press, 1948.

Chan, Sucheng. This Bitter-Sweet Soil. Los Angeles: University of California Press, 1986.

Chinn, Thomas W. (ed.) A History of the Chinese in California. San Francisco: Chinese Historical Society of America, 1969.

Clark, Thomas D. Frontier America. New York: Charles Scribner's Sons, 1959.

Cole, Martin and Welcome, Henry (eds.). Don Pio Pico's Historical Narrative. Glendale, California: The Arthur H. Clark Company, 1973.

Constable, George. (ed.). The Trailblazers. Alexandria, Virginia: Time-Life Books, 1973.

Current, Richard N., Freidel Frank, and Williams, T. Harry. American History: A Survey. New York: Alfred A. Knopf, 1967.

Daniels, Jonathan. The Devil's Backbone. New York: McGraw-Hill Book Company, 1962.

DeVoto, Bernard. The Year of Decision, 1846. Boston: Little, Brown and Company, 1943.

Dillon, Richard H. The Gila Trail: The Texas Argonauts and the California Gold Rush. Norman, Oklahoma: University of Oklahoma Press, 1984.

BIBLIOGRAPHY

Dillon, Richard. <u>Captain John Sutter: Sacramento Valley's Sainted Sinner.</u> Santa Cruz, California: Western Tanager Press, 1967.

Donald, David and Randell, J.G. <u>The Civil War and Reconstruction.</u> Boston: D.C. Heath and Company, 1961.

Donald, David H. <u>Lincoln</u>. London, Johathan Cape, 1995.

Dowdey, Clifford and Manarin, Louis H. (eds.). <u>The Wartime Papers of R.E. Lee.</u> Boston: Little, Brown, and Company, 1961.

Drury, Clifford M. <u>Marcus and Narcissa Whitman and the Opening of Old Oregon.</u> Glendale, California: The Arthur H. Clark Company, 1973.

Drury, Clifford M. <u>Marcus Whitman, M.D.</u> Caldwell, Idaho: The Caxton Printers, Ltd., 1937.

Egan, Ferol. <u>The El Dorado Trail.</u> New York: McGraw-Hill Book Company, 1970.

Ellis, Joseph. <u>Founding Brothers</u>. New York: Alfred A. Knopf, 2001.

Ellis, Joseph. <u>His Excellency George Washington</u>. New York, Alfred A. Knopf, 2004.

Etter, Patricia. <u>To California on the Southern Route, 1849.</u> Spokane, Washington: The Arthur H. Clark Company, 1998.

Evans, George W.B. <u>Mexican Gold Trail.</u> San Marino, California: The Huntington Library, 1945.

BIBLIOGRAPHY

Ferguson, Rebecca N. The Handy History Answer Book. Detroit: The Visible Ink Press, 2000.

Foote, Shelby. The Civil War: Fort Sumter to Perryville. New York: Random House, 1958.

Forbis, William H. The Cowboys. Alexandria, Virginia: Time-Life Books, 1973.

Freehling, William W. The Road to Disunion. New York: Oxford University Press, 1990.

Garraty, John A. The American Nation. New York: Harper & Row, 1966.

Garrison, Webb. Brady's Civil War. Guilford, Connecticut: The Lyons Press, 2000.

Gillenkirk, Jeff, and Motlow, James. Bitter Melon: Inside America's Last Rural Chinese Town. Berkeley, California: Heydey Books, 1987.

Goodwin, Doris Kearns. Team of Rivals. New York: Simon and Schuster. 2005.

Grant, Ulysses S. Grant. The Civil War Memoirs of Ulysses S. Grant. New York: A Tom Doherty Associates Book, 2002.

Greeley, Horace. An Overland Journey. New York: Alfred A. Knopf, 1964.

Grun, Bernard. The Timetables of History. New York: Simon & Schuster, 1982.

Hafen, Leroy R., Hollon, W. Eugene, and Rister, Carl, Coke.

BIBLIOGRAPHY

<u>Western America</u>. Englewood Cliffs, New Jersey: Prentice-Hall, Inc., 1970.

Hagedorn, Hermann. <u>The Roosevelt Family of Sagamore Hill</u>. New York: The Macmillan Company, 1954.

Hagerty, Donald J. <u>Desert Dreams: The Art and Life of Maynard Dixon.</u> Layton, Utah: Gibbs-Smith Publisher, 1993.

Hague, Harlan and Langum, David J. <u>Thomas O. Larkin.</u> Norman, Oklahoma, University of Oklahoma Press, 1990.

Handlin, Oscar. <u>America: A History.</u> New York: Holt, Rinehart and Winston, 1968.

Hardeman, Nicholas Perkins. <u>Wilderness Calling.</u> Knoxville, Tennessee: The University of Tennessee Press, 1977.

Harwell, Richard B. (ed.). <u>The Civil War Reader</u>. New York: Mallard Press, 1957.

Hittell, Theodore. <u>History of California.</u> San Francisco: Pacific Press Publishing House, 1885.

Holbrook, Stewart, H. <u>The Old Post Road.</u> New York: McGraw-Hill Book Company, Inc., 1962.

Holiday. J.S. <u>The World Rushed In.</u> New York: Simon and Schuster, 1981.

Hollon, W. Eugene. <u>Beyond the Cross Timbers.</u> Norman, Oklahoma: University of Oklahoma Press, 1955.

Hollon, W. Eugene. <u>The Southwest: Old and New.</u> New York: Alfred A. Knopf, 1961.

BIBLIOGRAPHY

Horsman, Reginald. The Frontier in the Formative Years, 1783-1815. New York: Holt, Rinehart and Winston, 1970.

Hunt, Thomas. Ghost Trails to California. New York: Weathervane Books, 1976.

Isaacson, Walter. Benjamin Franklin: An American Life. New York: Simon and Schuster, 2003.

Johnson, William Weber. The Forty-Niners. Alexandria, Virginia: Time-Life Books, 1974.

Karolevitz, Robert F. Newspapering in the Old West. Seattle, Washington: Superior Publishing Company, 1965.

Klose, Nelson. A Concise Study Guide to the American Frontier. Lincoln, Nebraska: University of Nebraska Press, 1964.

Kowalewski, Michael. (ed.). Gold Rush: A Literary Exploration. Berkeley, California: California Council for the Humanities, 1997.

Lamar, Howard R. (ed.). The Reader's Encyclopedia of the American West. New York: Thomas Y. Crowell Company, 1977.

Lapp, Rudolph M. Blacks in Gold Rush California. New Haven: Yale University Press, 1977.

Latta, Frank F. Joaquin Murrieta and his Horse Gangs. Santa Cruz, California: Bear State Books, 1980.

Levy, JoAnn. They Saw the Elephant. Hamden, Connecticut: Archon Book, 1990.

BIBLIOGRAPHY

Lothrop, Gloria Ricci and Nunis, Doyce B. Jr. (eds.) <u>A Guide to the History of California.</u> New York: Greenwood Press, 1989.

Maino Jeannette Gould. <u>Left Hand Turn: A Story of the Donner Party Women.</u> Modesto, California: Dry Creek Books, 1987.

McCullough, David. <u>1776.</u> New York: Simon and Schuster, 2005.

McDonald, Archie P. <u>William Barrett Travis: A Biography.</u> Austin, Texas: Eakin Press, 1995.

McPherson, James M. <u>Battle Cry of Freedom.</u> New York: Ballantine Books, 1988.

Miller Francis Trevelyan. (ed.). <u>The Photographic History of the Civil War in Ten Volumes.</u> New York: The Review of Reviews Co., 1911.

Mitchell, Broadus. <u>Heritage from Hamilton.</u> New York: Columbia University Press, 1957.

Moore, Joseph E. <u>Murder on Maryland's Eastern Shore</u>. Charleston: The History Press, 2006.

Morgan, Ted. <u>Wilderness at Dawn.</u> New York: Simon & Schuster, 1993.

Morris, Edmund. <u>Theodore Rex</u>. New York: The Modern Library, 2002.

Muir, Andrew Forest. <u>Texas in 1837.</u> Austin: University of Texas Press, 1958.

BIBLIOGRAPHY

Myres, Sandra L. (ed.) Ho for California! San Marino, California: Huntington Library, 1980.

Nadeau, Remi. Ghost Towns & Mining Camps of California. Santa Barbara, California: Crest Publishers, 1965.

Nevin, David. The Texans. Alexandria, Virginia: Time-Life Books, 1975.

Nevins, Allan. Fremont: Pathmarker of the West. Lincoln, Nebraska: University of Nebraska Press, 1939.

Newell, Chester. History of the Revolution in Texas. New York: Arno Press, 1973.

Nunis, Doyce B. (ed) The Bidwell-Bartleson Party: 1841 California Emigrant Adventure. Santa Cruz, California: Western Tanager Press, 1991.

Nunis, Doyce B. (ed) The Founding Documents of Los Angeles: A Bilingual Edition. Los Angeles: The Zamorano Club, 2004.

O'Brien, Cormac. Secret Lives of the First Ladies. Philadelphia: Quirk Books, 2005.

Paul, Rodman. Mining Frontiers of the Far West, 1848-1880. New York: Holt, Rinehart and Winston, 1963.

Pitt, Leonard. The Decline of the Californios. Berkeley: University of California Press, 1966.

Pomeroy, Earl. The Pacific Slope. New York: Alfred A. Knopf, 1966.

Rolle, Andrew F. California: A History. New York, Thomas Y. Crowell Company, 1963.

BIBLIOGRAPHY

Rolle, Andrew. John Charles Fremont. Norman, Oklahoma: University of Oklahoma Press, 1991.

Schlesinger, Arthur, M. Jr. The Cycles of American History. Franklin Center, Pennsylvania: The Franklin Library, 1986.

Schlissel, Lillian. Women's Diaries of the Westward Journey. New York: Schocken Books, 1982.

Seagraves, Anne. Soiled Doves: Prostitution in the Early West. Hayden, Idaho: Wesanne Publications, 1994.

Secrest, William B. California Desperadoes. Clovis, California: Word Dancer Press, 2000.

Secrest, William B. Lawmen & Desperadoes. Spokane, Washington: The Arthur H. Clark Company, 1994.

Secrest, William B. Perilous Trails, Dangerous Men. Clovis, California: Word Dancer Press, 2002.

Shirer, William L. The Rise and Fall of the Third Reich. New York: Simon and Schuster, 1960.

Slatta, Richard W. Cowboys of the Americas. New Haven: Yale University Press, 1990.

Smithwick, Noah. The Evolution of a State or Recollections of Old Texas Days. Austin: University of Texas Press, 1987.

Sosin, Jack M. The Revolutionary Frontier, 1763-1783. New York: Holt, Rinehart, and Winston, 1967.

Starkey, David. Six Wives: The Queens of Henry VIII. New York: Harper Collins Publishers, 2003.

WWW.TWISTINTIME.COM

BIBLIOGRAPHY

Starr, Kevin. <u>California.</u> New York: The Modern Library, 2005.

Steckmesser, Kent Ladd. <u>The Westward Movement: A Short History</u>. New York: McGraw-Hill Book Company, 1969.

Stewart, George R. <u>The California Trail.</u> New York: McGraw-Hill Book Company, Inc., 1962.

Stone, Irving. <u>Clarence Darrow for the Defense.</u> New York: Doubleday and Company, Inc., 1941.

Stone, Irving. <u>From Mud-Flat Cove to Gold to Statehood.</u> Clovis, California: Quill Driver Books, 1999.

Stone, Irving. <u>Men to Match My Mountains.</u> New York: Doubleday & Company, 1956.

Stone, Ted. <u>100 Years of Cowboy Stories.</u> Red Deer, Alberta, Canada: Red Deer College Press, 1994.

Tanner, Ogden. <u>The Ranchers</u>. Alexandria, Virginia: Time-Life Books, 1977.

Trachtman, Paul. <u>The Gunfighters.</u> Alexandria, Virginia: Time-Life Books, 1974.

Turner, Frederick Jackson. <u>The Frontier in American History.</u> Franklin Center, Pennsylvania: The Franklin Library, 1977.

Turner, Frederick Jackson. <u>The United States 1830-1850.</u> Gloucester, Massachusetts: Peter Smith, 1958.

Wallace, Robert. <u>The Miners.</u> Alexandria, Virginia: Time-Life Books, 1976.

BIBLIOGRAPHY

Webb, Walter, Prescott. History as High Adventure. Austin: The Pemberton Press, 1969.

Werner, M. R. "William Jennings Bryan: The Last Battle." America: An Illustrated Diary of its Most Exciting Years. Valencia, California: American Family Enterprises, Inc., 1973.

Wharton, Clarence. History of Fort Bend County. San Antonio, Texas: The Naylor Company, 1939.

Wheat, Frank. California Desert Miracle. San Diego, California: Sunbelt Publications, 1999.

Wheeler, Keith. The Railroaders. Alexandria, Virginia: Time-Life Books, 1973.

Whitsell, Leon O. One Hundred Years of Freemasonry in California. San Francisco: Griffin Brothers, Inc., 1950.

Worcester, Don. Pioneer Trails West. Caldwell, Idaho: The Caxton Printers, Ltd. 1985.

Young, Judy, Dockery and Young, Richard. Outlaw Tales. Little Rock, Arkansas: August House Inc., Publishers, 1992.

INDEX

A

Adams, Abigail 38
Adams, Charles 30
Adams, John 29; 37; 54
Adams, John Quincy 31; 56; 58; 60
Anderson, Major Robert 113
Arlington National Cemetery 121
Arthur, Chester 49
Astor, John Jacob 202
Atzerodt, George 144

B

Baghmati River 233
Bancroft, H.H. 152
Barron, Lieutenant William 31
Battle of Vienna 235
Bayard, James 55
Bear Flag Revolt 180
Bobbies 237
Boone, Daniel 26
Boone, Rebecca 27
Booth, John Wilkes 101; 128
Boston Massacre 10
Boston Tea Party 10
Braddock, General 44
Bradford, Mary 6
Bradford, Thomas 6
Bradford, William 5
Brannan Samuel 177
Brigham Young 162
Buchanan, James 79
Bull Run 124
Bunel, Joseph 40
Buntline, Ned 172
Burnham, Daniel H. 216

INDEX

Burr, Aaron 53
Burrows, Julius Caesar 178
Butler, General Benjamin 141

C

Calcutta, India 233
Calhoun, John 65; 60
Callender, James 42
Cameron, Simon 88
Campbell, Clarence 185
Carey, Matthew 25
Carter, Jimmy 93
Cass, Lewis 79
Charles I 245
Charles II 245
Chase, Kate 118
Chase, Salmon 139; 88
Chef Boyardee 223
Cheyenne Dog Soldiers 173
Chicago World's Fair 216
Chief Tanacharison 35
Chief Teneya 164
Churchill, Jennie Jerome 239
Churchill, Winston 214; 240
Clay, Henry 60
Cleveland, Grover 85
Coconut Grove Ball Room 208
Cody, William Frederick 172
Cody, Wyoming 173
Colton Hall 152
Colton, Rev. Walter 154
Corbett, Sergeant Boston 129
Corey, Giles 3
Corey, Martha 3
Crapper, Thomas 218
Crawford, William H. 60

WWW.TWISTINTIME.COM

INDEX

Crittenden, John J. 27
Cromwell, Oliver 245
Cumberland River 107
Custer, George Armstrong 168
Czar Nicholas II 212

D

De Jumonville, Monsieur 35
Delaware River 13
Detroit Red Wings 185
Difiance, Missouri 27
Donelson, Rachel 62
Donner Party 171
Dutch Harbor 194

E

Eaton, Peggy 65
Eiffel, Gustave 216
Eisenhower, Dwight David 189
Elkins, Stephen B. 178
Emancipation Proclamation 70
Evans, Billy 93

F

Fancher Wagon Train 162
Field, Maunsell B. 140
Folsom, Frances 87
Folsom, Oscar, 85
Ford's Theatre 128
Fort Bliss 230
Fort Bridger 160
Fort Donelson 107
Fort Henry 107

INDEX

Fort Moultrie 113
Frankfort, Kentucky 27
Franklin, Benjamin 21; 22; 44
Franklin, William 20
Freeman, William 90

G

Garfield, James A. 118; 82
Garfield, Lucretia 117
Geer, Elizabeth 158
George Washington 12; 14
Gettysburg 109
Gettysburg Address 73
Gibbons, Abby Hopper 137
Gitt, Georgie 72
Goddard, Robert 196
Grant, Ulysses S. 107
Gray, Peter 198
Great Wall of China 157
Greeley, Horace 147
Griffith Stadium 92
Guiteau, Charles 80

H

Hamlin, Hannibal 83
Hart, Peter 114
Harvard 29-30
Hefner, Hugh 7
Helm, Benjamin Hardin 105
Helm, Emilie Todd 105
Hemings Sally 41
Herold, David E. 144
Hershey, Milton 109
Hessians 12; 17
Hiss, Alger 205

INDEX

Hitler, William Patrick 248
Hood, General John B. 132
Houdini, Harry 191
Hudson River 12

I

Ide, William 180

J

Jack the Ripper 242
Jackson, 'Mudwall" 112
Jackson, Andrew 18; 60; 62; 64
Jackson, Colonel William L. 111
Jackson, General "Stonewall" 112
Jackson, Rachel 62
Jefferson, Thomas 41; 54
Jenkins, Robert 243
Johnson, Andrew 100; 140; 143; 84
Johnston, General Joseph E. 132

K

Kaiser Wilhelm II 212
Kennedy, Joseph Sr. 205
Kessler, Major J.M. 111
King George (III) 13
King George V 212
King George's War 244
King, William Rufus 78
Kiska 195
Kitty Hawk, North Carolina 221
Know Nothing Party 131

L

INDEX

L'Ouverture, Toussaint 39
Langley, Samuel P. 221
Lee, Alice Hathaway 96
Lee, John D. 162
Lee, Robert E. 110
Lewis, Meriwether 42
Lincoln, Abraham 67; 70; 73; 74; 76; 84; 88; 100; 106; 126
Lincoln, Mary Todd 74
Lippincott, Benjamin S. 152
Little Kanawha River 111
Louis XVI 236
Lovell, James 37

M

MacArthur, General Arthur 122
MacArthur, General Douglas 123
Madison, James 42
Manhattan cocktail 240
Manifest Destiny 67
Marie Antoinette 236
Mark Twain 175; 150
Marland, William C. 210
Marthasville, Missouri 26
Maxwell House 95
Mayflower 5
McCarthy, Joe 204
McClellan, General George 83; 100
McKinley, President William 192; 99
Meade, General 110
Meagher, Thomas Francis 130
Mencken, H.L. 227
Missionary Ridge 122
Monroe, James 17
Mountain Meadows Massacre 163
Mudgett, Ebenezer 10

INDEX

Mumford, William 141

N

Nast, Thomas 34
New Hampshire 10
New Jersey 12
New York Times 196
Nixon, Pat 201
Nixon, Richard 50; 201
Noyes, John Humphrey 80

O

O'Neal, Peggy 65
Old Thornburgh 160
Oneida Community 80
Ottoman Turks 235
Our American Cousin 89

P

Paine, Lewis 144
Pancho Villa 229
Parris, Betty 4
Parris, Reverend Samuel 4
Patton, General George S. 187
Patton, George S. 134
Peale, Charles Willson 14
Peale, James 14
Peel, Robert 238
Penicillin 209
Pershing, General John J. 229
Philadelphia Athletics 92
Pickens, Governor Francis 114
Pierce, Franklin 78
Plymouth Colony 6

INDEX

Pocahontas 9
Polk, James Knox 59
Presidio 230

Q

Queen Victoria 212

R

Richard, Maurice 186
Robards, Lewis 62
Rockwell, Norman 225
Rolfe, John 9
Roosevelt, Alice Lee 192
Roosevelt, Colonel Theodore 220
Roosevelt, Kermit 206
Roosevelt, Martha Bulloch 96
Roosevelt, President Franklin 225; 194
Roosevelt, President Theodore 94; 96; 98; 115
Royall, Anne 56
Royall, Major William 56

S

Salem Witchhunt 3
Sam Clemens 175; 150
San Domingo 40
Sanderson, James 59
Savage, Major James 164
Schallenberger, Moses 170
Schrank, John F. 98
Scott, Sir Walter 59
Separatists 5
Seward, Frederick 70
Seward, William H. 70; 88; 90
Sheridan, General Philip A. 122

INDEX

Sickles, General Daniel 106
Smith, Captain John 9
Smithsonian Institution 221
South Weare 10
St. Louis Browns 198
Stamp Act Revolt 10
Stanford, Leland 156
Stanton, Edwin 143
Stevens-Murphy party 170
Strobridge, James 156
Surratt, Mary 143
Sutter's Fort 170

T

Taft, William H. 92
Tennessee River 107
Titanic 203
Townsend, John 170
Trenton, Battle of 13
Troy, New York 33
Truman, Harry S. 167
Tyler, John 59

U

U.S. Fifth Cavalry 173
Uncle Sam 33-34

V

Vallejo, General Mariano 180
Van Nest, John 90

W

War of Jenkins' Ear 244

INDEX

Washington Martha 51
Washington Senators 92
Washington, Booker T. 39
Washington, Captain William 17
Washington, George 36; 49; 51
Weems, Parson Mason Locke 25
Weiss, Ehrich 190
Wentworth, Governor John 10
Wheeler, Joe 120
William Penn 109
William Todd 180
Williams, Abigail 4
Wilson, Henry 124
Wright, Orville 221
Wright, Wilbur 221

Y

Yosemite Valley 164
Young, Solomon 166

Bill Coate is the author of the Twist in Time series: *Twist in time: "History's Mysteries Revealed," Twist in Time: "History's Shocking Secrets"*, and *Twist in Time: "History's Outrageous Oddities."* He is a national award-winning historical author, educator and speaker.

Bill Coate founded the *Madera Method*—named by his mentor, renowned author, Irving Stone—a primary source research program for elementary students and the *Madera Method Wagon Train*, which takes students along the historic western wagon trails.

Bill was named *"National History Teacher of the Year"* by the Daughters of the American Revolution, received the *Disney American Teacher Award* and was a *"California Teacher of the Year"* finalist.

Bill is a resident of Madera, California. His historical vignettes are syndicated on television and radio and appear in several daily newspapers.